The Assessment of Special Educational Needs: Whose Problem?

THE EFFECTIVE TEACHER SERIES

General editor: Elizabeth Perrott

For series list see pages xxi–xxii

The Assessment of Special Educational Needs: Whose Problem?

DAVID GALLOWAY
DERRICK ARMSTRONG
SALLY TOMLINSON

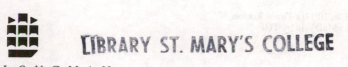

LONGMAN
London and New York

Longman Group UK Limited
Longman House, Burnt Mill
Harlow, Essex CM20 2JE, England
and Associated Companies throughout the world.

Published in the United States of America
by Longman Publishing, New York

First published 1994

ISBN 0 582 085144 PPR

British Library Cataloguing-in-Publication Data

A catalogue record for this book is
available from the British Library

Library of Congress Cataloging-in-Publication Data

Galloway, David, 1942–
    The assessment of special educational needs: responses to
emotional and behavioural difficulties / David Galloway, Derrick
Armstrong, Sally Tomlinson
        p.   cm. -- (The Effective teacher series)
    Includes bibliographical references (p.) and index.
    ISBN 0-582-08514-4
    1. Handicapped children--Education--Evaluation. 2. Mentally ill
children--Education--Evaluation. 3. Problem children--Education--Evaluation. 4. Special
education. 5. Education and state.
I. Armstrong, Derrick, 1953– . II. Tomlinson, Sally, III. Title. IV Series
LC4015.G25 1994
371.91--dc20   93-39141
                                                                          CIP

Set by 7E in 10/11pt Times Roman
Printed in Malaysia by TCP

CONTENTS

EDITOR'S PREFACE

This well established series was inspired by my book on the practice of teaching (*Effective Teaching: a Practical Guide to Improving your Teaching*, Longman, 1982), written for trainee teachers wishing to improve their teaching skills as well as for in-service teachers, especially those engaged in the supervision of trainees.

Although many of the books in this series have been written with a similar readership in mind, recent changes in the nature and pattern of education have led to the expansion of the series to include titles of importance to a wider readership such as head-teachers, parents, other educational professionals and those undertaking advanced study of education.

As specialists in their selected fields, the authors have been chosen for their ability to relate their subjects to the needs of the education profession as well as to stimulate discussion of contemporary educational issues among a wider audience.

The series aims to cover subjects ranging from the theory of education to the teaching of mathematics and from the assessment of special educational needs to effective teaching with information technology. It looks at aspects of education as diverse as education and cultural diversity and pupil welfare and counselling. Although some titles such as legal context of teaching and the teaching of history are specific to England and Wales, the majority of subjects such as teaching of statistical concepts and teaching as communication are international in scope.

Elizabeth Perrott

In the 15 years since publication of the Warnock Report provision for special educational needs (SEN) has become a matter for intense educational and political debate. Head teachers, school governors and parents take a keen interest in decisions about the allocation of resources, *and* in decisions about individual children. Yet in spite, or perhaps because, of the fact that SEN has a higher profile now than at any time in the past, it is also the focus for greater controversy and dissatisfaction. As more groups – parents, politicians and a wide range of professionals – take greater interest, the only thing that becomes clear is that every aspect of provision for SEN is deeply shrouded in ambiguity. The concept itself is hopelessly confused: can a 'special' need be a 'normal' response to stressful circumstances at home or at school? Should we concentrate on *educational* needs when our principal concern may be with the child's *social* background? *Whose* needs are we addressing?

No aspect of provision for SEN arouses stronger feelings that its assessment. Controversy does exist over the techniques and methods used in assessment, but the principal concern, both for professionals and for parents, is not over which test or assessment technique should be used, but over something much more complex, namely the context in which assessment takes place, and the effect this has on parents, children and professionals.

We knew from our previous experience and from the professional literature that many parents were dissatisfied with the processes involved in assessing children's SEN under procedures in the 1981 Education Act. So, for different reasons, were many teachers and other professionals. Discussion with teachers and educational psychologists suggested that the context in which assessment takes place can create tensions for everyone involved, whether as professional or client. 'Context' includes the hopes and expectations of all participants regarding the outcome of the process. How far these hopes and expectations are met depends, in complex and often unpredictable ways, on constraints arising from policy at school, LEA and government levels. Policy decisions create constraints which result in participants having different, and often conflicting, hopes and expectations. As our preliminary discussions unfolded, we realised that there was remarkably little research on how different professional participants – for example, teachers, educational psychologists, clinical medical officers (school doctors) or social workers – saw their task and resolved tensions arising from it. Nor had there been much work on how parents and children saw the process. More important, even less work had been done on how different participants in the assessment of children's SENs might come to see the same process from different, often conflicting, perspectives. We therefore applied to the Economic and Social Research Council for support to enable us to investigate in detail the assessment of emotional and behavioural difficulties (EBD) under provision in the 1981 Education Act, as seen by professionals and by clients.

Why 'emotional and behavioural' difficulties?

Our reasons for concentrating on EBD were both theoretical and pragmatic. First, children with emotional and behavioural difficulties arouse strong feelings in the teachers who work with them. Second, it is clear that the number of children whose behaviour is defined as 'unmanageable' appears to be increasing. This is reflected in anecdotal accounts of dramatic increases in the number of children excluded from school or referred for assessment under the 1981 Act on account of their difficult behaviour. It is also reflected in the government's last-minute decision to insert a clause in the 1993 Education Act requiring LEAs to make special provision for disruptive pupils. Third, the concept of EBD is value laden and context specific. Extensive research, together with the professional experience of most teachers, is in agreement that children can behave in quite different ways in different situations. Children do not always behave in the same way with all teachers, nor do all teachers agree on the behaviour they regard as acceptable or otherwise. Yet no other group of SENs is more likely to be attributed to problems in the child's home background. Fourth, the overlap between behavioural problems and learning difficulties is well documented. Children referred to support services on account of difficult behaviour are often educationally backward, but the relationship between learning and behavioural problems is not straightforward. In these circumstances, differences in interpretation between professionals, as well as between professionals and parents, become almost inevitable. EBD epitomises the tensions inherent in the assessment process. We felt that if we could throw light on mutual understandings and misunderstandings between professionals, parents and children in as complex an area as the assessment of EBD, this could have implications for the assessment of children with other sorts of learning difficulty.

The research

We studied in detail the process of assessing 29 children who had been referred on account of emotional and behavioural difficulties. Whenever possible we observed interviews related to the assessment, for example, between educational psychologists and parents, and psychologists and children. We also attended clinical medical officers' examinations of children, and talked at length to head and class teachers. Subsequently we talked to each participant – professionals and clients – separately to elicit and discuss their perceptions of the purpose of each interview and what it had achieved. Table 0.1 summarises our database.

Table 0.1 Summary of database

Assessment interviews observed		Researchers' interviews with participants	
Psychologist's interview with child	18	Parents	51
Psychologist's interview with parents	24	Children	33
Psychologist's interview with teachers	12	Psychologists	60
		Clinical medical officers	20
Welfare officer's interview with parents	6	Teachers (mainstream school)	46
		Teachers (special school)	14
Case conferences	13	Social workers	7
Statutory medicals	12	Educational welfare workers	5
Court hearings	2	Psychologists	1
Classroom observations	6	Administrators/LEA advisers	4

For further details see Galloway *et al.* (1992)

All participants were volunteers. Rightly, professionals questioned us closely about our aims and methods, and our own credentials, before agreeing to take part. The project sought and received approval from the Ethical Committee of no fewer than six district health authorities.

We had a two-stage procedure for seeking co-operation from parents. First, we discussed the requirements of the research in general terms with senior officers of the LEA. This discussion concentrated on the presenting problems thought to be characteristic of EBD. At this stage we were usually given verbal outlines of possible cases, with all identifying characteristics removed. The purpose of this was to prevent disproportionate representation of a particular age-group or a particular sort of presenting problem. An officer of the LEA then made contact with the parents (whose identity we still did not know), giving them a letter explaining the purpose of our research and asking if they would be willing to take part. If they agreed, and only five did not, we were given their names and addresses. At the second stage we visited the homes of the parents to explain in person the purposes and scope of the project, and to satisfy ourselves that they and, wherever practicable, the child were giving their informed consent. Parents were asked to agree in writing to take part, but retained a copy of the letter, explaining that they could withdraw at any time simply by informing us or any professional person involved in the assessment of their child. No parent withdrew at stage 2, and only one parent withdrew subsequently.

The methodology was labour-intensive, and occasionally stressful. Inevitably we became aware of highly sensitive information about families, and parents and children occasionally unburdened themselves to the visiting researcher. So, we should add, did professionals. They, too, were acutely conscious of pressures and tensions arising from a complex and often contradictory process which might have profound implications not only for a child's educational future but also for their own relationships with other professional colleagues. We always made clear, and constantly reiterated, that we had no involvement in any decisions arising from a child's assessment. Yet there were times when both parents and professionals sought to enlist our support for a particular course of action. In retrospect this was perhaps inevitable; if you talk to people about something important they have experienced, the discussion is likely to help them to clarify their views, and this cannot always be divorced from enlisting support for them. The ethical and professional dilemmas in ethnographic research are becoming increasingly well known. Our approach was to address the problem openly and explicitly whenever it arose. This did not always altogether resolve the problem, but we do not believe that the outcome of any child's assessment would have been different had we not been involved.

Structure of the book

In Part I we analyse the context in which SENs are assessed, and try to unravel the respective influences of school, LEA and government policy. In Part II we examine the process from the perspectives of children, parents and educational psychologists. The school's perspective is implicit in each of these. Although our research started *after* the school had decided to request a formal assessment – and this is a limitation which we acknowledge – interviews with teachers revealed the complex and often acute pressures that had led to referral and which influenced their beliefs about an appropriate outcome. In Part III we look beyond our own material in an analysis of problems and possibilities in multidisciplinary assessment.

We have already noted that participants differed in how they saw the assessment of SEN. Responses to our research have differed just as widely. In evaluating research projects that it has supported, the Economic and Social Research Council sends copies of final reports to independent referees with an acknowledged reputation in the subject. One wrote dismissively that the topic of our research needed 'sustained investigation but, on the basis of the present offering, by a different team'! Another wrote that '... this seems to me an excellent study, which is well-planned and executed'. We were not particularly surprised by these divergent views. Research in areas of education policy should not aim at a cosy consensus; rather it should aim to stimulate lively and constructive debate. We hope that our book will contribute to this debate.

NOTE ON AUTHORSHIP

Planning and writing this book was a cooperative venture. Inevitably, though, there was some division of responsibilities. Each chapter went through at least two drafts as we took account of each other's criticisms. For the record, Chapters 1, 2 and 10 were written mainly by David Galloway, Chapters 4, 5 and 9 by Derrick Armstrong, Chapters 7 and 8 by Sally Tomlinson and Chapters 3 and 6 by David Galloway and Derrick Armstrong.

ABBREVIATIONS

AC — Audit Commission

BoC — Board of Control

BoE — Board of Education

CACE — Central Advisory Council for Education

CMO — Clinical Medical Officer

DES — Department of Education and Science

DFE — Department for Education (formerly DES)

EBD — Emotional and Behavioural Difficulties

GCSE — General Certificate of Secondary Education

GMS — Grant Maintained School

HC — House of Commons

HMI — Her Majesty's Inspectors of Schools

ILEA — Inner London Education Authority

LEA — Local Education Authority

LMS — Local Management of Schools

SED — Scottish Education Department

SEN — Special Educational Need(s)

Acknowledgements

The research described in this book was carried out with support from the Economic and Social Research Council for Grant No. R000 23 1393 . . . The Assessment of Emotional and Behavioural Difficulties: Participant Perspectives. The project was directed by David Galloway and Sally Tomlinson. The Research Associate who did most of the fieldwork was Derrick Armstrong.

We are also grateful to the necessarily anonymous LEAs; district health authorities and social services departments which gave permission for the research to take place. In addition we acknowledge with respect and appreciation the willingness of teachers, educational psychologists, LEA education officers, clinical medical officers, social workers and other professionals who allowed us to observe their work and, often in moments of pressure, found time to talk to us about it. Finally, we acknowledge with similar respect and appreciation the agreement of parents and their children to take part in the research. They allowed us to observe aspects of the assessment process which were often sensitive and sometimes painful. They, too, found time to talk to us about their experience of this process. The fact that professionals and their clients did not always share the same perspective should not obscure the high level of integrity which they both showed in their willingness to discuss in depth their respective experiences of the assessment of emotional and behavioural difficulties.

The publishers are indebted for permission to reproduce copyright material.

The Association for Child Psychology and Psychiatry for extracts from the article 'Who is the Child Psychologist's Client? Responsibilities and Options for Psychologists in Educational Settings' by Derrick Armstrong and David Galloway from *ACCP Newsletter* Vol 14, No 2 (1992); Carfax Publishing Company for an extract from the article 'The Assessment of Special Educational Needs and the Proletarianisation of Professionals' by Derrick Armstrong, David Galloway and Sally Tomlinson from *British Journal of Sociology of Education*, extracts from the article 'Assessing Special Educational Needs: the child's contribution' by Derrick Armstrong, David Galloway and Sally Tomlinson from *British Educational Research*

Journal Vol 19, No 2 (1993) and extracts from the article 'Decision-making in the Psychologists Professional Interviews' by Derrick Armstrong, David Galloway and Sally Tomlinson from the journal *Educational Psychology in Practice* Vol 7, No 2, (1991); Routledge for an extract based on the chapter 'On being a client, conflicting perspectives on assessment' by Derrick Armstrong and David Galloway from *Policies for Diversity in Education* Edited by T Booth et al (pub Routledge/Open University)

List of Figures and Tables

Disclaimers

When presenting case histories and when quoting verbatim from parents, children or members of any of the professional groups who took part in the research described in this book, we have changed names, abbreviations of names, nicknames and any other identifying characteristics. The views expressed in this book are those of the authors and should not be taken to reflect those of their employers, or of individuals or institutions who cooperated in any of the inquiries referred to in the book.

TEACHING AS COMMUNICATION by Bob Hodge

THE ASSESSMENT OF SPECIAL EDUCATIONAL NEEDS: WHOSE PROBLEM? by David Galloway, Derrick Armstrong and Sally Tomlinson

THE EFFECTIVE TEACHING OF SECONDARY SCIENCE by John Parkinson

PART I

The context for assessment

CHAPTER 1

The origins and meaning of special educational needs

Introduction

The 1980s witnessed a minor revolution in public and professional interest in special educational needs (SEN). This was reflected in the time allocated to SEN by schools, by HMI and by local education authority advisory and inspection services. In the 1970s it was unusual for HMI reports to allocate more than a brief paragraph to SEN. Today virtually every report allocates a substantial section to the resources provided and the effectiveness of the teaching. If children in the 1970s, were experiencing learning or behavioural difficulties in a mainstream school there was, in most LEAs, a straight choice: leave them in the school and hope that teachers would be able to give them some additional help without any additional resources, or recommend their transfer to a special school, at which they would almost certainly remain until they left school. In contrast today resources for SEN are based on a dual funding system:

(a) Resources can be specified on the 'Statement' of a child's SEN issued under provision of the 1981 Education Act.
(b) The 1988 Education Reform Act requires LEAs to allocate an annual budget to each school, as part of the Local Management of Schools (LMS), and the formula for determining the size of this budget must include provision for SEN.

As a result, resources for SEN have become a matter of interest and concern to head teachers and LEA administrators. As the overall power of LEAs to influence policy and practice in schools has declined as a result of the Conservative Party's antipathy to local government, the importance of SEN provision relative to all other functions performed by the LEA has increased. There are two principal reasons for the increasing importance of provision for SEN. First, the 1981 Education Act gave parents certain rights to request, and to participate in, the assessment of their children's SEN and to appeal against LEA decisions. Second, and partially as a result of this, the associations representing specific interest groups have become better organised and more vocal. Parents of children with special needs now have greater access to reliable information and high-quality support from voluntary groups than at any time in the past. There are, however, certain notable exceptions, for reasons which we explain later in the book. Parents of children with generalised learning difficulties which are not associated with 'dyslexia', or with emotional and behavioural difficulties, still have limited access to independent advice.

Yet in spite of greater awareness of SEN and of the allocation of resources specifically for SEN in mainstream schools, dissatisfaction with SEN provision has probably never been greater, both from parents and from head teachers. The problem does not lie principally in their evaluation of the effectiveness of the resources that have been provided, though there are strong reasons for asking how much provision does actually 'meet' the special needs of the pupils for whom it is intended. Rather, dissatisfaction focuses on the processes of assessing special needs and of determining the resources to be made available.

Superficially, assessment might appear a straightforward process: a child either has a physical disability requiring special educational help or he or she does not; similarly, another child either has a learning or a behavioural problem requiring special provision, or he or she does not. In practice the process is anything but straightforward. There are three interrelated issues.

1. Assessment provides the key to resources, and resources are never infinite; with some justification, parents and head teachers regard them as something to be fought for. LEA administrators often regard them as something to be fought *over*.
2. Whether children are regarded as having SEN depends at least in part on the quality of the teaching and the resources their schools are able to provide. We shall return to this issue in Chapter 3. All we need to note here is that children's progress, or lack of progress, and behaviour results from complex interactions in which the school plays an important part.
3. Assessment is primarily a political and social process and, as in any political and social process, misunderstandings occur and polarised positions may be adopted.

The final point merits further discussion. The fact that teachers and educational psychologists use a variety of educational attainment tests and 'intelligence' tests in their assessment of learning difficulties does not make the process objective. The tests themselves have a substantial margin of error. The more important issue, though, concerns the differing, and sometimes conflicting, assumptions which provide the context in which they are used, and the differing expectations which determine how the results are interpreted. These assumptions and expectations may include beliefs about the causes of the child's problems, about the adequacy of the teaching he or she is currently receiving, about the possibility of overcoming the difficulties in question, and about the best sort of provision for children with special needs. Throughout this book we shall be drawing on our research to illustrate the critical issues that lie behind a decision to carry out an assessment of SEN, as well as the critical issues in the process itself. The remainder of this chapter will examine how provision for SEN has developed since the 1944 Education Act. We shall then focus on assessment as a political and social process before analysing the meaning of the concept of SEN. Briefly, we shall consider why LEA and school policies for SEN provision so often appear arbitrary and inconsistent.

The development of SEN provision

Concern about a large minority of children with learning and/or behavioural difficulties has a long history which is both consistent and confused. The consistency lies in conclusions about the size of the 'problem'. The Wood Committee regarded about 10 per cent of children as retarded, even though they did not technically fill the (rather vague) criteria for certification as feeble minded (BoE/BoC, 1929). Researching behaviour problems, McFie (1934) reported a remarkable 46 per cent of pupils as showing at least one 'behaviour deviation' while an even earlier American study reported undesirable behaviour in over 50 per cent of pupils (Haggerty, 1925). Clearly, neither learning nor behavioural difficulties are peculiar to the 1980s and 1990s.

We can interpret the concern about these children in several ways. Special provision, either in the mainstream or in a special school or unit, can be seen as a humanitarian response to the needs of children with problems. Yet special educational provision also reflects anxiety about the effect which the children concerned may have on other children. This concern can be seen from two perspectives. First, the eugenics movement was influential in promoting the view that people of inferior intelligence and/or morals – in practice these were often conflated – should be segregated from the rest of society, partly for their own good and partly to prevent them from passing on their allegedly degenerate characteristics to the next generation by breeding. Second, with large classes and, by today's standards, hopelessly limited resources, mainstream teachers demanded action on behalf of children who at best were failing to learn, and at worst were seriously disrupting the other pupils.

The 1944 Education Act introduced universal secondary education, based on selection by ability at age 11. A major extension to the scope of special educational provision was perceived as necessary if the new secondary schools were to operate successfully. The justification, and the means of selecting children, was provided by evidence from psychologists, notably Cyril Burt (see Hearnshaw, 1979). They claimed that children could be assessed at 11 as suitable for education in a grammar, technical or secondary modern school. Using similar procedures, they could be assessed as requiring special education.

The Act created categories of handicap, and if a child was 'ascertained' as 'suffering' from one of these categories, the LEA was required to provide special educational 'treatment' in a special school or class recognised for the purpose. Assessment was the responsibility of school medical officers, who were trained by leading psychologists to administer the Stanford Binet Intelligence Test. One reason for this was pragmatic: LEAs simply did not employ enough educational psychologists to carry out the necessary assessments. Another reason was that learning and behaviour problems were still seen essentially as medical rather than educational matters.

In the 30 years following the 1944 Act it gradually dawned on educationalists and on senior school health personnel that the categories of handicap told them nothing about a child's *educational* needs. One of the Department of Education and Science's senior school medical officers referred privately to the 'crude, naive and lazy simplicity of terms like educationally sub-normal and maladjusted'. The categories gave teachers no guidance to help them in subsequent work with the child. Indeed, because they were based on quasi-medical criteria, it was not even clear that the child did in fact have special *educational* needs. At the same time training courses for educational psychologists were starting to meet a growing demand from LEAs. This resulted in tension between school doctors and educational psychologists as the latter challenged the doctors' competence in educational assessment. Tomlinson (1981a) has described the competition for clients in which psychologists asserted their expertise in what had previously been a medical preserve.

The issue was largely resolved by 1974 when Margaret Thatcher, as Secretary of State for Education and Science, appointed Mary Warnock as Chair of a committee whose brief was:

to review educational provision in England, Scotland and Wales for children and young people handicapped by disabilities of body, or mind, taking account of the medical aspects of their needs, together with arrangements to prepare them for entering into employment; to consider the most effective use of resources; and to make recommendations. (DES, 1978, p.1)

Membership of the committee reflected the dominance of professional views on the education of children with special needs. Of the 26 members, only one was the parent of a child with a handicap. No black person was invited to serve, nor was any person with a handicap. The only non-specialist outside the civil service, the teaching profession and the support services was Mary Warnock herself – at the time an Oxford philosophy don – and even she was a former head teacher. The message was clear: professionals would decide what was best; parents might be welcome as partners, but could not be expected to have the necessary knowledge or experience to make any substantial contributions to the committee's work.

In 1975, three years before the committee submitted its report, the DES issued non-statutory guidelines to LEAs which radically changed the procedures for assessing SEN. These placed educational psychologists at the centre of the process, with a key role in advising the LEA about the child's educational needs. Formal ascertainment was only to be used when the LEA considered that special school placement should be enforced against parental wishes.

The Warnock Report recommended abolition of the 1944 Act's categories of handicap, and their replacement with the generic concept of special educational needs (DES, 1978). Drawing on a wide range of epidemiological and longitudinal research, the report recommended that services should be based on the assumption that up to 20 per cent of children would have some form of special educational needs at some stage in their school career, and up to 15 per cent at any one time. Thus, the scope of special educational provision was broadened from the 2 per cent who had received special educational treatment under the 1944 Act to include around 20 per cent of the population. The 'problem' of SEN thus became indistinguishable from the 'problem' of low achievement and pupil behaviour generally. In the same year an influential report by HMI in Scotland sought to extend the concept still further by arguing that up to 50 per cent of children had learning difficulties, and that mainstream teachers should be catering for them (SED, 1978).

The consequence of extending the concept of SEN was to stimulate debate and discussion in all mainstream schools. As an awareness-raising exercise this may have been useful. We shall argue, though, that in the long term it has had profound and unhelpful consequences for the assessment of SEN.

The government's response to the Warnock Report was the 1981 Education Act. This had two essential functions: first, to provide a legislative framework for provision for SEN, based on those aspects of the Warnock Report with which the government agreed; and, second, to do so without providing any new resources from central funds. The 1944 Act categories were finally abolished, and replaced with the generic concept of special educational needs. Children with learning difficulties who were thought to require special provision beyond what was normally available in their mainstream schools should receive formal and multidisciplinary assessment to determine whether they did in fact have SEN. If the reports indicated that the child did have special needs, the LEA would issue a 'statement', specifying the nature of the needs, how and where they should be met, and the resources that should be made available. Parents were given the right to appeal against an LEA decision to carry out an assessment and against a decision not to issue a statement following an assessment. They were also given the right to discuss a 'Proposed Statement' with a named officer of the LEA before it was formally issued. Subsequently they could appeal against a formally issued Statement to a local appeals committee and, finally, to the Secretary of State. (Technically, the last resort is an appeal to the European Court of Human Rights, but the child will most probably have left school before the appeal is heard.) The assessment and appeal procedures both involve an intimidating amount of paper work which have been referred to cynically as 'a bureaucrat's dream' and 'a parent's nightmare' (Galloway, 1985).

The 1981 Act was essentially an enabling Act. Although the procedural requirements were specified in detail, it left LEAs with extensive autonomy in deciding what provision should be made. As with the Warnock Report, the 1981 Act was based on a professional consensus on what constituted good practice. It is widely assumed that the Act encouraged the integration of children with special needs into mainstream schools. In fact, the commitment to integration is remarkably weak, noting merely that children should be taught in ordinary schools subject to:

- parental wishes
- the possibility of meeting the child's needs in an ordinary school
- 'provision of efficient education for the children with whom he will be educated'
- the efficient use of resources.

Galloway and Goodwin (1987, p.21) note that:

the last two choices could have been invoked for every child ever placed in every special school in the country. Once an LEA has separate special schools it is obviously 'inefficient' not to use them. Further, many children with learning or adjustment problems are referred *because* of their effect on other children.

Swann (1985) analysed DES statistics from 1978 until 1982, the last full year before the 1981 Education Act came into force. The figures showed an increase in children placed in schools specialising in 'moderate' levels of intellectual handicap. The picture since the Act came into operation in April 1983 is confused as the DES has altered the way it collects statistics. Nevertheless, the Centre for Study of Integration in Education has argued that by no means are all LEAs adopting a policy of integration (Swann, 1992). In the case of children who present behavioural difficulties, it is likely that provision outside the mainstream continued to increase throughout the 1980s.

Emotional and behavioural difficulties (EBD) remained one of the most frequent reasons for referral to special schools. The 1981 Act abolished the 1944 Act's category of maladjusted, and the concept of EBD merely reflected official recognition that the children concerned would have to be described, or categorised, in some other way. At the same time the amount of provision for children regarded as 'disruptive' was continuing to increase. As early as 1980 the Advisory Centre for Education published a survey in which just over half the LEAs cooperated. Places existed for 6791 pupils, or around half the number in schools for 'maladjusted' children. The distinction between children who were labelled 'disruptive' and children who were said to be 'maladjusted' is instructive. Prior to the 1981 Act, children ascertained as maladjusted had to be placed in a school recognised for that category. LEAs discovered in the 1960s and 1970s that it was cheaper and administratively easier to open a unit or centre for problem pupils than provide a special school. The reasons lay in the small print of the 1944 Act and need not concern us here. The point, though, is that children placed in centres or units could not be labelled maladjusted since to do so would require special school placement. Hence, an alternative term was needed. LEA administrators and many educational psychologists strove valiantly to convince themselves that 'disruptive' and 'maladjusted' children were two clinically distinct groups requiring different forms of provision. This was nonsense. The distinction was a bureaucratic necessity which had nothing to do with the children or their problems. In the 1970s and early 1980s David Galloway assessed over 100 severely disruptive pupils following their exclusion from school. Without exception, a case could have been made out for labelling each of these pupils 'maladjusted' if it would have served any useful purpose to have done so. While all pupils labelled 'disruptive' could have been defined as 'maladjusted', the reverse was not necessarily the case. Some children categorised as 'maladjusted' could not readily have been labelled 'disruptive' – for example children who were exceedingly timid, fearful or withdrawn at school or at home.

In theory, the 1981 Act overcame the need for assessment of special needs to make the spurious distinction between children who were disruptive and children with emotional and behavioural difficulties. The Act placed no restrictions on how special needs were defined. Having identified the child's needs, the LEA has virtually unlimited powers, subject to parental agreement, in deciding how and where to meet them. In practice, old habits die hard. Many professional reports recommending special school placement continue to refer to emotional and behavioural difficulties, while 'disruptive' is more often used when seeking admission to a part-time or short-term centre or unit.

The Fish Report (ILEA, 1985)

Its explicit basis on a professional consensus on good practice was a strength of the Warnock Report, but also a limitation. Warnock provided a framework for the assessment of special needs, but had little to say about the educational context in which they became apparent. As part of a wider review of its education service, the Inner London Educational Authority commissioned a review of SEN provision from John Fish, a former chief of HMI for special education. This report started to broaden the debate by identifying provision for SEN as an important aspect of the authority's politically high profile policy on equal opportunities:

the aims of education for children and young people with disabilities and significant difficulties are the same as those for all children and young people. . . . Disabilities and significant difficulties do not diminish the right to equal access to, and participation in, society. (Para. 1.1.22)

The report also recognised explicitly that the expectations of other people could be critical in determining the extent to which disabilities and difficulties became handicapping. From here it was a fairly short step to the recommendation that

all teachers accept responsibility for meeting as far as possible the special educational needs which may arise in their classroom, and be enabled to do so in collaboration with the network of advisory and support services available to them. (Para. 3.16.20)

While the Fish Report has been deservedly influential, it failed to recognise the relevance of research on school and teacher effectiveness. If, as we argue in Chapter 3, some schools contribute to the learning and behavioural difficulties which are taken as evidence of SEN, whereas other schools have a protective influence, then any assessment of a child's needs must take into account the context in which those needs have become apparent.

The context includes the contribution of the teacher as an individual. Teachers vary in their tolerance level for learning and behavioural difficulties. The also vary in *what* behaviour they find disturbing. Thus, one teacher may be seriously upset by a verbally aggressive child while another may regard this as a relatively minor irritant. Similarly, one teacher may regard a child's lack of progress in reading with relative equanimity, while another may regard it as a matter for serious concern. The reaction will depend on the teacher, and on the expectations of the teacher's senior colleagues, the child's parents and the local community. In this sense, teachers 'construct' special needs. However, the construction of special needs is also influenced by wider political, economic and social processes.

Assessment as a political and social process

The implication of the last paragraph is that whether a child's attainments or behaviour are seen as evidence of SEN depends in part on what parents, employers and the government expect from the education system. Lack of progress in reading is seen as a greater problem by some parents than by others. The individual's perception, though, is certain to be influenced by wider cultural and economic considerations.

Of children referred to educational psychologists for assessment and advice, a high proportion have some form of reading difficulty. A few children are referred because of their problems with maths, but very few are referred because they show neither interest nor aptitude in subjects such as art, music and even science. Knowledge is socially 'constructed' in the sense that what constitutes knowledge varies according to the priorities of a particular culture at a particular time. In primary schools creative arts are more highly valued today than before the changes associated with the Plowden Report (CACE, 1967). Nevertheless, literacy remains the issue that most concerns teachers and parents, largely because so much else depends on it. Within the memory of at least two authors of this book, all the brightest pupils at leading grammar and public schools were expected to learn Greek. The dominance of classics remained unchallenged until the early 1960s. Today Latin and Greek are minority subjects, and in many schools have been replaced at the top of the 'status order' by maths and natural sciences.

Just as knowledge is socially constructed, so is lack of knowledge. Britain's crudely élitist examination system is based on the failure of a majority of pupils (Fontana, 1984). GCSE and 'A' levels act as an efficient filter in ensuring that only a select minority achieve the qualifications that act as a passport to higher education. Moreover, Britain still produces a large minority of leavers with no qualifications, though the introduction of GCSE has reduced this. A consistent claim from the right wing of the Tory Party has been that while we compare well with our competitor countries in Europe and elsewhere in the achievements of the most able 20 per cent of pupils, we compare badly in the achievements of those pupils Sir Keith Joseph so uninspiringly referred to as the 'bottom 40 per cent'. While the picture is not altogether clear, there is some evidence for this view (e.g. Prais and Wagner, 1986; Prais, 1986).

Does it matter now, and has it mattered in the past? The answer is less obvious than it might appear. For some 30 years after 1945, Britain enjoyed reasonably consistent, if uneven, growth and a steadily improving standard of living. Certainly, there were massive inequalities within society, with widespread poverty in many areas. On the other hand, the unemployment figures would make today's politicians envious, and in the 1950s Harold Macmillan sailed to election victory on the message that: 'You've never had it so good.' School-leavers with no qualifications could confidently expect jobs in the country's traditional industries, such as steel, mining or ship-building. Then, as now, schools were expected to produce young people with the knowledge, skills and attitudes needed by the employment market – that included young people with few qualifications, or none, whose expectations were unskilled or semi-skilled manual jobs. Bluntly, the economy required a workforce of ex-pupils who might today be regarded as having had special educational needs.

Of course, this could not be stated publicly. The 1944 Education Act was firmly committed to the liberal ideology of secondary education for all. Education was *ipso facto* desirable, holding the key to personal fulfilment as well as national prosperity. Yet for most pupils, the liberal dream remained nothing more than a dream. The better independent and grammar schools offered a curriculum that guaranteed entry to high status and relatively well paid jobs, while giving pupils the grounding for a life-long interest in the arts. For many more young people, though, education was a socialisation process, preparing them for repetitive, mostly manual jobs. In the words of the title of a classic in the sociology of education, it was about *Learning to Labour: How Working Class Kids get Working Class Jobs* (Willis, 1977). Numerous accounts attest to the educational and cultural limitations of life for many pupils in secondary modern schools and the early comprehensives (Blishen, 1955; Hargreaves, 1967).

Yet education remained a politically uncontroversial matter. The main parties disagreed on details, but their commitment to an overall expansion in educational opportunities was not in doubt. This consensus, resulting at least in part from general economic stability and relatively full employment, provided no political incentive to meddle with the curriculum. The 1944 Act stipulated only one compulsory subject: religious education. In Britain, national and local politicians publicly exerted less direct control over the curriculum than in any other country. The curriculum became known as the 'secret garden' which neither politicians nor the public might enter.

There were two further reasons for the autonomy granted to teachers. First, it was always assumed that they would use their autonomy conservatively not radically, producing the young people needed by the employment market, and not introducing contentious or radical ideas into the curriculum. Second, the grammar schools created by the 1944 Act were modelled largely on the public school system, in which the head master's (sic) autonomy over the curriculum had never seriously been challenged. Hence, there was no tradition in the country's élite schools of political intervention in the curriculum.

This cosy consensus could not last. By the mid-1970s Britain was starting to enter a post-industrial economy, and by the end of the recession of the early 1980s the country's industrial base had undergone a radical change. Far from being needed by the economy, school-leavers with low educational attainments and no qualifications were a drain on it. They faced almost certain unemployment and the dole was expensive. Worse, their anger and resentment threatened to cause social unrest; by 1981 the threat of riots in some inner city areas had become a reality.

The implications for the education system were recognised by politicians in both main parties. In a seminal speech at Ruskin College, Oxford, James Callaghan (1976) questioned the education system's achievements and asserted that it was not adapting to the requirements of a changing economy. At the same time educationalists and politicians on the right of the Conservative Party were publishing polemical articles with a more strident tone, but a not dissimilar message (e.g. Cox and Boyson, 1977). Pupils with low achievements were becoming a source of political concern.

Defining special educational needs

It will be apparent from the argument so far that criteria for defining SEN are culturally determined. Whether a child's educational attainments are regarded as evidence of learning difficulties depends largely on what the dominant authority expects children to achieve. Whether a child's behaviour is seen as a problem depends on how children are expected to behave. For the Victorians, the well-behaved child was seen but not heard. Today, the same child might be referred to a psychologist as withdrawn or as having communication difficulties. What sense, then, can we make of the term SEN?

A starting point is to ask how the Warnock Committee reached their conclusion that up to 20 per cent of pupils would have some form of special educational needs at some stage in their school career. At one level, it was simply a political compromise based on a statistical artefact (Galloway, 1985). The committee had access to research which reported the prevalence of various educational and behavioural problems. Prevalence was defined in terms of pupils' scores on intelligence and attainment tests for educational problems, and in terms of questionnaires or rating scales for behavioural problems. The intelligence and attainment tests were designed to ensure a reasonably even distribution of responses above and below the mean. The questionnaires and rating scales enquired about problems commonly experienced by teachers, for the rather obvious reason that they were designed for completion by teachers. Warnock's 20 per cent was a statistical artefact in the sense that the committee could have identified *any* proportion of children as having special educational needs, while pointing to the same research studies to justify their conclusion. The difference would have been based solely on where they placed the cut-off points. In this sense the figure is also a political compromise. In the same year, HMI argued that up to 50 per cent of pupils in Scottish schools could be said to have learning difficulties (SED, 1978), and a few years later Sir Keith Joseph was expressing concern about the 'bottom 40 per cent'. The proportion of children attending special schools was about 2 per cent, so if the committee wished to introduce an extended concept of special educational needs they could select from 2 to 50 per cent. Twenty per cent was a compromise, likely to be accepted by the government and welcomed by the profession, as a figure which illustrated the scale of the problem without necessarily implying the need either for excessive additional resources or for radical redefinition of current educational priorities.

The term 'special educational needs' nevertheless remains confused on philosophical grounds, with no agreed criteria for its use. There are two principal problems. One concerns the meanings which are implicit in the term but are seldom made explicit. The second concerns the criteria for using the term or, more often, for not using it.

Each of the three words *special*, *educational* and *needs* raises its own questions. 'Special' is defined in the Oxford dictionary as: 'of a peculiar or restricted kind'. While that may be true of children with severe and complex difficulties, it is obviously not true of the mainstream school pupils to whom the term could be applied. As we have just argued, Warnock extended the term to include the large minority of low-achieving and mainly working-class pupils whose education became politically contentious with the economic changes in the late 1970s. Far from being special, there is a powerful argument that the children's needs were absolutely normal, and that the challenge for the school system was, quite simply, to start meeting them. There is certainly no sense in which the pupils' needs were 'restricted'; indeed, part of the logic of the National Curriculum was that their curriculum had been too restricted in the past. Nor could they be called 'peculiar' since a political imperative, shared by both parties, was to extend the knowledge and skills they had acquired by the time they left school.

The word 'educational', at first sight, appears less contentious. Warnock was, after all, emphatic in rejecting the medically based categories of the 1944 Act on the grounds that they told us nothing about a child's educational needs. Yet this conflates educational needs with other needs which may be more important for the child's educational progress. If children are living in stressful circumstances at home, this may affect their motivation, behaviour and work at school. Certainly, there will be implications for the school, but these may concern the need for stability, a supportive relationship with a teacher, a sense of achievement from extra-curricular activities, and so on. To say the child has special *educational* needs may be, at best, misleading.

Finally, the concept of 'needs' implies that something is wanted. Logically, we cannot say we need something without in some sense wanting it. Even a potentially painful visit to the dentist implies a wish to be free from real or threatened pain. Superficially, when we say a child has special educational needs we imply that we want something for, or on behalf of, the child. This may be true, but children with learning and behavioural difficulties are a source of stress in the classroom. In saying a child has special educational needs teachers may be implying, not unreasonably, that *they* want a less disruptive life, or that they want *other* children's education to benefit from the child's removal. In other words, the 'wants' implied in the concept of special educational *needs* may not refer to the child in question.

Discourses of 'needs'

Confusion over the term 'special educational needs' has a parallel in similar confusion over criteria for its use. The problem is not essentially one of identifying criteria, but rather of deciding when the term is appropriate. As the 'problem' of widespread low and/or under-achievement came to be recognised by politicians and by the media, three areas of discourse emerged about the causes and the solutions. Only one of these acknowledged the concept of special educational needs. Yet it is only if we recognise the relevance for this concept of the other two discourse areas that we can see the tensions inherent in it.

The 'special needs pupil' discourse

The implication in Warnock's conclusion that up to 20 per cent of children may have special educational needs is simple. The committee was implying that teachers ought to be able to cope with around 80 per cent of pupils with no extra help, but could reasonably expect some extra support with the remaining 20 per cent. The argument was clearly predicated on the notion of help for the individual child. It was consistent with a liberal ideology of concern for the unfortunate and disadvantaged. Any definition of special educational needs would clearly have to include low- and/or under-achieving pupils, as well as pupils with emotional and/or behavioural difficulties. The implication of the 'special needs pupil' discourse is that the children, or their teachers, should be offered some special support, probably on an individual or small group basis. Clearly, in order to determine what form this special support should take, a careful assessment must be carried out of the individual's requirements.

The 'school and teacher effectiveness' discourse

Research on school effectiveness has demonstrated the impact of schools on their pupils' progress and behaviour, arguing that differences between schools cannot be attributed merely to differences in the pupils' social and educational backgrounds (e.g. Rutter *et al.*, 1979; Mortimore *et al.*, 1988; Smith and Tomlinson, 1989). The educational implication is that problems of low achievement and difficult behaviour may have as much to do with curriculum delivery, pedagogy and school climate as with the pupils themselves. Research on teacher effectiveness, too, supports the view that the quality of learning experience is likely to play an important part in pupils' educational progress. A well-known study investigated the match in primary schools between the difficulties of the task and the pupil's ability (Bennett *et al.*, 1984), finding that many teachers tended to set tasks which were too difficult for their less able pupils and too easy for the more able. The focus, though, is on the teacher's work with the class, rather than with children selected for special help. There is little in the school and classroom effectiveness discourse to suggest that problems should be solved by giving pupils special work on an individual or small group basis.

The 'school failure' discourse

This is essentially a political variant of the school and teacher effectiveness discourse. It is illustrated in political concern about the 'bottom 40 per cent', and sees the problem as a reflection of poor teaching and outdated ideology.

Overview

There is extraordinarily little explicit recognition that each of these three areas of discourse is concerned with the same socially constructed problem. At least 10 of Warnock's 18 per cent form part of Joseph's 40 per cent, all of whom could be included in the Scottish Education Department's 50 per cent. Nevertheless, each discourse attributes the problem to different factors, and each heads in different directions.

The 'special needs pupil' discourse is essentially individualistic, attributing learning difficulties to factors in the pupil and in the pupil's family and social background. It implies the need for special resources attached to named pupils. The school and teacher effectiveness discourse, in contrast, explicitly acknowledges that learning and behavioural problems may be attributable, at least in part, to tensions in curriculum delivery, pedagogy or school climate. It leads to calls for professional development and in-service training as ways of promoting school improvement. It is essentially a professional discourse: 'Give us the support and the resources, and we'll do the job.' Finally, the school failure discourse demands radical legislative reform, since the teaching profession is considered unable or unwilling to reform itself.

Conclusions

The three discourse areas show how different people can talk about the same problem from different perspectives. These different perspectives involve different ways of conceptualising the range of issues which are seen as evidence of special educational needs. Unfortunately, this conceptual confusion on the causes and nature of the problem, as well as on the solutions, is evident in the 1981 Education Act, in the 1988 Education Reform Act, in the 1993 Education Act and in many LEA and school policies. In their evidence to the House of Commons Education, Science and Arts Committee (HC, 1987), HMI maintained that few LEAs had a coherent policy on special educational needs, and of the few which did, even fewer had a coherent plan for implementing their policy. Perhaps this is not altogether surprising. It does, nevertheless, indicate the importance of understanding the social consequences of identification of special needs.

CHAPTER 2

The 1988 Education Reform Act: liberator or albatross?

Introduction

In this chapter we examine the politics of the 1988 Education Reform Act and the implications of the Act for provision for special educational needs. SEN is hardly mentioned in the Act itself, yet the implications both for the amount and for the nature of provision are profound. Moreover, it is clear that a major aim of the Act was to raise the standard achieved by many of the pupils Warnock would have regarded as having special needs. Unfortunately, the Act was confused and inconsistent in the way it conceptualised special needs. We shall analyse the sources of this confusion and illustrate its consequences, drawing on evidence from our own research. Finally, we shall argue that confusion within the Act has been compounded by the inadequacy and inconsistency of policy on special educational needs in many LEAs.

Special educational needs and the 1988 act: central or marginal?

Special educational needs are hardly mentioned in the 1988 Act. Section 19 gave head teachers the power to modify or disapply the national curriculum in circumstances subsequently spelled out by the Secretary of State (DES, 1989c). The National Curriculum can also be modified or disapplied by a Statement issued under the 1981 Act. By confining references to special needs to procedures for exempting pupils from the requirements of the National Curriculum, the government appeared to be signalling that special needs were at most of marginal concern in its education reform. The reality was quite different.

All the Act's principal clauses have direct or indirect implications for provision for special needs. More important, the underlying aim of raising educational standards was firmly based on the 'school failure' discourse referred to earlier (p. 16). Once we accept that 20 per cent of pupils may have special educational needs at some stage in their career, let alone the 40 per cent of 'low-achieving' pupils recognised by Sir Keith Joseph or the 50 per cent with learning difficulties referred to by HMI in Scotland (SED, 1978), we also have to accept that the effectiveness of provision for special educational needs is integrally linked to that of the education system as a whole. In other words, special educational needs had become a matter of political debate. By including low standards in the rationale for educational reform, the government was politicising provision for special needs.

The 'special needs pupil' discourse (p. 15) attributes learning difficulties to problems in the children or their families. This analysis conflicted with that of the government, which attributed low and/or under-achievement to poor teaching and an inappropriate curriculum. This could not, however, be stated openly; not even the third and fourth consecutive Tory governments dared openly to attack the principle of special provision for special needs. The 'school and teacher effectiveness' discourse might have been acceptable, but this discourse was based on the teaching profession's willingness and ability to reform itself from within. The government no longer accepted the profession's commitment to reform, nor was it willing to provide the resources the profession was certain to demand. Thus the problem of low and under-achievement was central to the rationale for the Act, but it was impossible openly to equate this problem with that of special educational needs, even though anyone who stopped to think would have had to recognise a massive overlap. Unfortunately, the government lacked the conviction of its own logic, and this led to some fatal inconsistencies. Before exploring these, however, we need to examine in greater detail the view that the Act was based on a political consensus.

Concensus between right and left?

No party in opposition could ever support radical new legislation. Yet the Labour Party's opposition to the 'Great' Education Reform Bill, derisively known by many teachers as the GERBIL, did not concentrate on questions of curriculum and assessment. The reason lay in a common conclusion that schools were failing a large minority of pupils.

A consistent theme in sociological research and theory has been that the education system maintains, even deepens, the existing divisions within society. In the 1960s a succession of reports argued that selection at 11 for grammar or secondary modern schools discriminated against working-class children (Douglas, 1964). With the introduction of comprehensive schools, a series of ethnographic studies identified differences in the quality of experience which different pupils received at school (Hargreaves, 1967; Lacey, 1970; Hargreaves *et al.*, 1975; Ball, 1981; Burgess, 1983). Consistently schools were seen to cater less adequately, both in educational and in social terms, for pupils in lower ability groups. The studies documented the potentially destructive impact of schooling on young people who rejected the values for which, they felt, the school stood, on the grounds that the school had first rejected them (Willis, 1977; Corrigan, 1979). In a seminal book, Hargreaves (1982, p.17) asserted that the secondary school system, mainly through the hidden curriculum, exerted on many pupils, mainly but by no means exclusively working class,

a destruction of their dignity which is so massive and so pervasive that few subsequently recover from it.

Warnock's committee saw at least 18 per cent of pupils as having special educational needs (the remaining 2 per cent of Warnock's 20 per cent had traditionally been taught in special schools). Hargreaves and others were concerned with the social consequences of schooling for a large minority of working-class pupils. Yet if they were not concerned with identical groups, the overlap was certainly massive.

Hargreaves' analysis was accepted enthusiastically by the left wing Inner London Education Authority (ILEA, 1984), but the right wing of the Tory Party had been expressing concern about the same pupils since the so-called Black Papers of the 1970s (eg. Cox and Boyson, 1977). The right-wing analysis claimed that standards were falling, particularly among less able pupils. In a speech to the Council of Local Education Authorities, Sir Keith Joseph (1983) announced that he was setting up the (less than inspirationally entitled) Lower Achieving Pupils Project:

It is my job as Secretary of State to remind partners in the education service that the education of lower attaining fourth and fifth year secondary pupils is one of the most pressing problems with which we need jointly to come to grips.

As the bandwagon for reform gathered pace, talk of partnership was rapidly forgotten. The Tory view, though, was neatly encapsulated by Boyson (1988, p.4):

We still do almost as well as competitor countries with the education of our top 20 per cent ability children. It is with the average and below average that we often do badly.

The right and the left may have agreed that schools were not serving low- and/or under-achieving pupils well, but they differed radically on the reasons. For the left, the problem lay in the denial of resources and opportunities to under-achieving children. More important, the school system inevitably reflected the interests of powerful groups within society, and hence was deeply implicated in maintaining and reproducing existing stratification based on class, race and gender, irrespective of the views of individual teachers (Bourdieu 1977).

The Tory analysis differed in fundamental respects. For them, the problem lay in the radicalism, not the conservatism, of teachers. Grace (1987, p.214) sums up the changing relationship between teachers and the state:

Radical teachers, especially in inner-city schools, were portrayed as militant trade unionists intent on industrial action and work-place democracy on the one hand and as cultural and ideological subversives intent on the politicisation of classroom practice on the other. These teachers, 'the trendies and the lefties', were, it was alleged, exploiting school and classroom autonomy to the full and for the wrong reasons.

Linked to this was the deep mistrust of allegedly disorganised, profligate 'looney left' local authorities which featured so prominently in Tory demonology in the 1980s and early 1990s. These LEAs were not only said to be wasteful in their use of resources and irresponsible in their approach to curriculum reform; they were also said to tolerate low standards which resulted in large numbers of young people leaving school without the skills and qualifications they would need in the employment market.

Suggesting that schools were controlled by rabid radicals was untenable. Teachers have always been as deeply conservative, in a non-political sense, as any other professional interest group. Recognising the absurdity of the 'looney left' critique, without ever denying its validity, the right broadened its attack. Schools were said to be élitist, concerned principally with an academic élite who would progress to higher education. Because these pupils were easier and more rewarding to teach, academically less able pupils were neglected (e.g. O'Keefe, 1987). The left could hardly disagree. The final part of the right wing critique was that teachers and other educational professionals were preoccupied with their own conditions of service at the expense of their pupils. This charge adapted the original image of teachers in hard-left LEAs as radical subversives, to portray them as willing to sacrifice their pupils in pursuit of ever-increasing salaries and resources. The prolonged industrial action over teachers' pay in 1986 was used by the government to prepare public opinion for the Education Reform Act two years later. Given the Tory's expressed aim of reducing public expenditure, a public concern for educational standards legitimised the conflict with entrenched professional interests.

If, then, the right and the left agreed that schools were failing to meet the needs of a large minority of pupils, even though they disagreed about the reasons, what were the implications? Galloway (1990a) has argued that they could agree on two implications. First, professional control over the curriculum should be reduced. Teachers might be the conscious or unconscious agents of socially and economically powerful interest groups. Alternatively they might, according to a right-wing analysis, be using their autonomy in the classroom in a radical and subversive way. In either case, the logical conclusion would demand a shift towards the centre in the balance of power, and the obvious way to achieve this would be by introducing a national curriculum.

Second, vested professional interests had consistently failed to respond to the changing demands of the economy, and hence had implicitly failed to meet pupils' needs or recognise the aspirations of their parents. One logical conclusion would be to give parents greater control over the choice of their child's school. Restriction on choice would maintain the existing stratification by preventing pupils living in socially disadvantaged areas from attending more 'successful' schools.

We have argued so far that both political parties could, logically, have supported the introduction of a national curriculum, and even, more controversially, of increased parental choice on the school their children should attend. We must now look at the probable impact on pupils with special educational needs.

The National Curriculum and national testing.

Professional interest groups were united in their opposition to the National Curriculum (Haviland, 1988). Politically, though, the curriculum could no longer remain a 'secret garden' in which professionals could bask safe from the prying eyes of the uninitiated. For the first time, the National Curriculum established the principle of a legally enforceable curriculum entitlement for all pupils. In theory, at least, it would no longer be possible to shunt pupils into a low-status 'non-academic' siding. This was a potentially important advance. Many primary and secondary schools catered for special needs by removing pupils from the mainstream for additional 'help', mainly in reading. Evidence for the effectiveness of withdrawal groups had always been limited, suggesting that progress made in the special group was often lost on return to the mainstream (see Galloway and Goodwin, 1987). In addition, curriculum development in secondary schools had tended disproportionately to focus on curricula for less able pupils, at least in part because the formal examination system did not place so many constraints on what, or how, these pupils were taught. The curricula were designed with the pupils' interests in mind, but sociological analyses showed that the pupils themselves perceived the special programmes as a way of removing them from the mainstream while teachers concentrated on more able students who were easier and more rewarding to teach (e.g. Hargreaves, 1982).

By 1992, the National Curriculum was largely in place in primary schools, and plans for its introduction throughout years 7–11, the secondary years, were well advanced. The principle of the National Curriculum was no longer contentious. Argument focused on the content of particular subjects (e.g. Cox, 1991) and on the demands it made of teachers (e.g. Alexander *et al.*, 1992), but the profession had largely accepted it as a permanent feature on the landscape.

The principle of national testing programmes, too, was largely accepted, though with much greater reluctance, and with bitter argument about the form they should take and the uses that should be made of the results. Initial anxiety centred partly on the risk of identifying pupils as failures from the age of 7, partly on the belief that parents might place intolerable pressure on their children to do well, and partly on the fear that publication of results would create a multi-tier system which would push some schools into a descending spiral as the more articulate and better informed parents sent their children elsewhere. Galloway (1990, p.59) commented:

There is a peculiar arrogance in supporters of a system which more or less compels parents to hand their children over to strangers for a major part of their lives from the age of 5, yet refuses to give them any precise information on what educational standards their children should have attained after a given time, let alone any objective guidance on their progress relative to other children. In the past, well informed and articulate parents have generally been able to obtain the information they wanted. Parents of children with learning and adjustment difficulties all too often have felt themselves left, or kept, in the dark. . . . At least the Act gives parents of children with special needs *some* information.

The decision to include virtually all pupils in national testing programmes is based on a particular perspective on special educational needs. The 'special needs pupil' discourse assumes that the children must first be identified, and then that specific programmes must be designed for them. In contrast, the 'school failure' discourse, and the 'school and teacher effectiveness' discourse, assume that children fail to achieve because they receive inappropriate teaching. Excluding these pupils from national testing would deny them the right to demonstrate their abilities. It would also reduce their teachers' accountability to parents or school governors.

This raises a further point about teacher accountability. The separation in the 1988 Act of the National Curriculum Council from the Schools' Examination and Assessment Council was an intentional device for separating the process of assessment from the process of curriculum development. The traditional view, followed by professionals, had been that assessment procedures could be worked out once the curriculum had been planned: let the experts decide what children should learn, and then decide how to assess it. The radical alternative, both for the left and for the right, demanded the opposite: decide what should be assessed in each curriculum area at different ages, and *then* plan the curriculum. It was not until the 1993 Act that the government felt sufficiently confident to unite SEAC and the NCC. By this time it believed that the power of a shadowy 'educational establishment' had been broken. No longer would curriculum experts be able to decide what should be taught. The impact on children with SEN could be seen in two ways: (a) they would have to sink or swim as best they might; (b) for the first time they were entitled to a full curriculum, and could no longer be condemned to a low-status alternative.

Open enrolment

By extending the 1980 Education Act, the 1988 Act prevented LEAs from rejecting parents' choice of school except on the grounds of space. This has placed schools in open competition with each other, as their annual budget depends mainly on pupil numbers. Clearly, freedom is unequally distributed, since parents who can afford the transport to take their children to schools some distance from home have greater choice than those who cannot. As a result there is an obvious risk of creating ghetto schools, attended by pupils whose parents have few educational aspirations and/or who cannot afford transport to the successful schools elsewhere.

Two further points should be made here. First, open enrolment is based on parental choice. The Conservative government has always professed a commitment to giving parents greater choice. The 1980 Education Act extended the information available to parents by requiring publication of public examination results and HMI reports, and by stipulating much of the information that schools should provide in their prospectuses. The 1988 Act further extended this process, but failed to acknowledge a critical weakness in the previous legislation. This was simply that information on school exam results is meaningless without information on the pupils' attainments when they entered the school. The same applies to the results of national testing programmes at 7, 11 and 14. Knowing how much *progress* children have made is more useful than knowing what standard they have achieved at a given time. By refusing to acknowledge the importance of 'value added' measures, insisting on publication of 'raw' scores, the government has insisted that parents be given misleading information. The position of schools on league tables of exam results can be transformed depending on what measure is used. More important, the government's chosen measure of raw scores discriminates in favour of schools with a middle-class pupil intake. The fact that the pupils tend to achieve higher scores in every age-group may conceal the evidence that they have actually made less *progress* than pupils in schools with a less privileged intake.

The second point concerns the market economy in which schools compete for pupils. This has made schools more conscious of their image with parents and in their local community. No school wants a reputation for low standards, nor for poor discipline. Two predictable consequences have been an increase in the number of pupils excluded on grounds of behaviour, and an increase in the number of pupils referred for assessment under the 1981 Act (AC–HMI, 1992). We shall analyse the reasons later. Here, we need only note that as schools become more and more image conscious, their willingness to cater for children with learning and/or behavioural difficulties may correspondingly decrease.

Local management of schools

Local management of schools (LMS) aimed to enable school governors to use resources more effectively. The annual budget was to be based on a formula largely determined by age-weighted pupil numbers, which should be 'simple, clear and predictable'. This requirement has caused some hilarity as heads and governors struggle to master the labyrinthine complexities of their LEA's LMS scheme. Nevertheless, the principle of LMS is not controversial, either educationally or politically, although there is widespread dissatisfaction with local procedures. Its impact on provision for special educational needs does, however, remain highly contentious. The question is always the same and concerns resources.

In mainstream schools, provision for special needs comes from three sources: (a) resources can be linked to a statement, and when this happens the LEA has a legal obligation to provide them; (b) LEAs can provide advisory and support services which are available to all schools; (c) the formula for determining the annual budget allocated to each school must contain an element for special educational needs. LEAs vary in their methods of calculation (Lee,1990): some include a sum based simply on pupil numbers, but a larger proportion make a rough estimate of the number of pupils with special needs in each school, normally by means of group tests of verbal reasoning and/or educational attainments, administered to all pupils in a particular age-group.

The proportion of all resources for special needs allocated to schools via the LMS formula, as opposed to resources held centrally to fund Statements and support services, varies widely from LEA to LEA and can have far-reaching consequences. If schools believe that the only way to obtain additional resources is to persuade the LEA to issue a Statement, the number of children referred for formal assessment is likely to escalate.

The special needs element in each school's annual budget is not 'earmarked': in other words, no commitments are placed on head teachers or governors in deciding how to use it. If they decide to use it to appoint an extra teacher to teach 'A' level Physics to a handful of high-flying pupils, there is nothing to stop them. There appears to have been little research on how schools actually use the special needs element in their budgets. In some LEAs, the amount involved in the largest schools can exceed £200 000. It would be an unusual school which targeted the whole sum at provision of *additional* support and resources for pupils with learning difficulties, irrespective of whether we use Warnock's criteria (DES, 1978) or those of the Scottish Education Department (SED, 1978). A far more usual approach appears to be to allocate a limited proportion to the school's own designated network of support for special needs, with a much larger proportion allocated to 'across the board' benefits for all pupils and staff – for example, a modest reduction in class sizes.

In theory, the way a school uses its funds is monitored by its own governors, by the LEA, by the occasional inspections required in the 1992 Education Act, and by HMI. In practice, governors rely heavily on professional advice from the head, and although LEAs are still able to inspect SEN provision on a regular basis, their powers are severely limited by the resources at their disposal. The role of HMI in monitoring standards and inspecting schools has been drastically altered by the 1993 Education Act, and there is, as yet, inadequate information on how the proposed new school inspection teams appointed by the Office for Standards in Education (OFSTED) will interpret their responsibilities in relation to special educational needs.

To counter this somewhat depressing picture, as schools become increasingly accountable to parents for pupils' progress, the progress of their less able pupils may assume greater importance. Moreover, if parents become better informed about their children's curricular entitlement under the National Curriculum, they may exert increasing pressure on schools to target resources more selectively.

Grant-maintained status

One of the most frequently heard arguments against legislation allowing schools to opt out of LEA control by seeking grant-maintained status (GMS) is that they will become less willing to accept pupils with special needs. Initially it appeared that this fear might be unfounded. Schools were required to specify their intended admission policies when applying for GMS, and no school was to be permitted to change its status for at least five years after obtaining grant-maintained status. The 1988 Education Reform Act, however, bestowed numerous new powers on the Secretary of State, for which no new parliamentary mandate is needed. By decree, and with no prior parliamentary debate, schools are no longer required to retain their previous status for five years, and the Conservative government now appears to be encouraging formerly comprehensive schools to seek permission to become grammar schools, or to specialise in certain areas of the curriculum. In either case, selective admission policies will be introduced. Following the Conservative victory in the 1992 election, and the subsequent issue of the 1993 Education Act, it became clear that the number of secondary schools seeking grant-maintained status was likely to rise sharply. This could result in pupils with learning or behavioural difficulties being concentrated in the few remaining LEA-maintained schools, or in grant-maintained schools that have not been granted specialist status.

Overview

As originally proposed by Kenneth Baker, Secretary of State for Education and Science in 1988, the Act held the potential for major advances in the funding of education for the low-attaining and/or under-achieving pupils about whom leading members of the Conservative Party had expressed so much concern. Sadly the Act gave the Secretary of State extensive powers which led to lack of consistency in policy and created the conditions for its own failure. The lack of consistency in policy is evident in the bewildering change in National Curriculum requirements and in the government's increasingly frequent and direct intervention in the work of the National Curriculum Council and the Schools Examination and Assessment Council. Education clearly *is* a political matter, but its quality will deteriorate rapidly if it becomes a political football, kicked not only in disputes between the two main parties, but also by different members of the ruling party as they use it to ingratiate themselves with different interest groups. However, the Act also contained more fundamental areas of confusion which have already undermined its professed aim of raising standards.

Confusion within the Act

We have already noted that the Act was implicitly based on the 'school failure' discourse. The rationale was simple: the professionals had failed; they were unwilling to reform themselves, so reform must be imposed by legislation. Life is seldom so simple. The critique on which the Act was based contained fatal inconsistencies.

Parental choice?

Concern about the consequences of low and/or under-achievement was genuine, though not necessarily altruistic. Its motivation lay in anxiety about the costs of unemployment and social unrest more than in a benevolent concern to extend educational opportunities. The concern was nevertheless genuine, but rested uneasily alongside a determination to give parents more information and more choice. Part of the commitment to choice lay in a thinly veiled commitment to encourage the return of grammar schools or other specialist secondary schools. These specialist schools included City Technology Colleges and 'magnet' schools specialising in designated areas of the curriculum. Parental opinion had been solidly against the reintroduction of grammar schools whenever it had been proposed by Tory LEAs. Tory voters were nevertheless thought likely to welcome the return of specialist secondary schools, and the comprehensive system was associated, quite unjustifiably, with the 'trendy lefty' teachers who featured so prominently in Conservative demonology.

The problem, of course, is that increasing choice for a few parents necessarily involves reducing it for others. It was always clear that grammar schools, like the early grant maintained schools, would be held to embody the traditional values of strict discipline and academic excellence. Because successive Secretaries of State rejected the idea of publishing league tables comparing pupils' *progress* in different schools (the so-called 'value added' criteria), this belief could not easily be challenged. It nevertheless ensured that other schools would be regarded as second class, with all the potential consequences for their success in attracting pupils with a wide range of abilities and from different social backgrounds. The return of specialist secondary schools seems likely to mean the return of a two-tier education system. This is a curious way to demonstrate commitment to raising the attainments of pupils in the second tier.

Which discourse?

Although the 1988 Act was motivated by the 'school failure' discourse, it lacked the courage of consistency. The 1981 Education Act was retained, with its commitment to a detailed multidisciplinary assessment to determine whether or not a child had special educational needs. Thus the key clauses of the 1988 Act, such as introduction of the National Curriculum, national testing and grant-maintained schools, were based on the belief that schools had failed, and only new legislation could raise standards. In contrast, special resources for children with severe or complex learning difficulties continued to be based on the 'special needs pupil' discourse.

Whereas LEAs are *permitted* to include an allowance in their LMS formula for social disadvantage in the school's pupil intake, they are *required* to include an element for special educational needs. There is little evidence of logic here. The procedures for determining the special needs element in the formula usually involve testing pupils' attainments, and hence reflect the school's own effectiveness, or that of its feeder primary schools when testing is carried out in the first term of secondary education. The more effective the school, the fewer pupils will fall below some arbitrarily defined criteria of special educational needs. Hence, there is an obvious risk of penalising good schools and rewarding bad ones. It would be more equitable to base the special needs element in the formula on indices of social disadvantage, since these are less dependent on the quality of teaching within the school.

Confusion in LEA policies

We have already noted HMI's evidence that few LEAs had a coherent policy on special educational needs (HC, 1987). The 1988 Act has prompted several LEAs to carry out reviews of their existing provision, but the whole area remains fraught with confusion. An important part of the problem lies in the apparent inability of most LEAs to establish clear and consistent criteria on which to base agreement to carry out formal assessments.

The Warnock Report advocated five stages in a child's assessment. These are summarised in Table 2.1 Stages 1–3 involve the school in carrying out a thorough analysis of the child's needs, including informal discussion with relevant members of the LEA's support services. The school would have attempted to plan and to implement an appropriate response to the problem, and would be able to provide detailed documentation of the steps that had been taken. Common sense might suggest that LEA officers would never agree to implement formal assessment procedures as specified in the 1988 Act unless they were satisfied that schools had fully implemented the steps in Warnock's stages 1–3.

Table 2.1 **Warnock's stages of assessment**

School-based assessments: Stages 1–3

Stage 1	Head teacher marshals information on child's performance
Stage 2	Discussion with specialist teacher with possibility of special programme supervised by this teacher
Stage 3	Informal assessment by professionals brought in by the head teacher or school doctor, e.g. educational psychologist

Multi-professional assessment: Stages 4–5

Stage 4	Assessment by professionals with direct responsibility for local services
Stage 5	If needed, assessment by experts with narrower specialism or geographically wider responsibilitites

---

We shall discuss head teachers' reasons for requesting assessment in the next chapter. Here, however, we are concerned with the judgements that LEAs make when they receive a request that they initiate formal assessment procedures. Our research suggests that the pressures on LEA officers are more complex than is often recognised, at least by teachers.

LEAs have to accept a 'reasonable' request for assessment. Most LEAs routinely agree to any request from parents. A large majority of requests, however, come from schools, and that raises questions about LEA criteria for starting the process. Some LEAs interpret *any* request from a school as *prima facie* evidence that an assessment is needed. An alternative position is to accept a request only if it is accompanied by documentary evidence showing that Warnock's first three stages have been followed. In theory, most LEAs have policies which state that schools should follow the internal and informal assessment procedures recommended by Warnock before starting the process leading to a Statement. In practice it is clear that these are often ignored.

Our research took place in three LEAs. In one, the stated policy was that requests for assessment would only be accepted if supported by the school's educational psychologist. Psychologists were expected to satisfy themselves that appropriate measures had already been taken to assess and to meet the child's needs without resorting to the cumbersome procedures of the 1981 Act. In a second LEA, head teachers submitted requests to a panel of senior officers. This panel routinely accepted almost all requests, and subsequently had responsibility for receiving professional reports and deciding what resources could be provided to meet the needs that had been identified. In the third LEA requests were directed to a divisional office, which routinely initiated the formal procedures.

In theory, then, only one of the three LEAs had explicit procedures designed to ensure that the preliminary informal stages had been followed. Of the 29 children whose assessment we studied, there was evidence of preliminary assessment procedures only in 7 cases. The criteria we used here was that some form of intervention had been implemented and evaluated before referral, following consultation between the class teacher, the special needs coordinator for the school, the head or deputy and an outside adviser. Clearly, the schools regarded all the pupils as having severe problems, and were usually, though not always, able to provide evidence of their difficult and disturbing behaviour. What was conspicuously missing in the majority of cases was any indication of discussion with specialist teachers about the possibility of a special programme for the child (Warnock stage 2) and informal assessment by relevant professionals such as educational psychologists (Warnock stage 3). We wondered whether schools had in fact been through these stages, but had not seen the need to describe them in their requests for 'Statementing' procedures. Our interviews with head and class teachers seldom revealed evidence that this was the case.

Even in the LEA which 'filtered' referrals through educational psychologists, there was not always evidence of school-based assessment before requesting the statutory procedures. The reasons lay partly in the reluctance of educational psychologists to question a head teacher's decision to request formal assessment. They felt that this could, at best, merely delay the process, while at the same time creating tensions in their relationships with schools. An additional reason was that reduction in staff was said to have made the informal decision and assessment advocated by Warnock impractical.

A LEA's criteria, or lack of criteria, for initiating formal assessment procedures reflect the way it conceptualises SEN. Returning to the three discourses described in Chapter 1, the 'school failure' discourse assumes that inadequate teaching may well have contributed to the problem. The logic of this discourse would require the LEA to scrutinise every application for Statementing procedures with great care, to ensure that schools had first made every possible effort to help the child and were not simply seeking to off-load a difficult pupil or to obtain extra resources. The same is true of the 'school and teacher effectiveness' discourse, though here the LEA would be more inclined to offer help from advisory services to enable teachers to respond more effectively to the child's needs. In contrast the 'special needs pupil' discourse implicitly assumes that the problem lies in preparing an individualised programme for the child, and consequently that professional effort should concentrate on an assessment of the individual's needs.

Both the 'school failure' discourse and the 'school and teacher effectiveness' discourse would be likely to lead the LEA into conflict with head teachers. Moreover, the 1986 Education Act confirmed that schools have the ultimate sanction of excluding pupils. The LEA does indeed have the power to order a pupil's reinstatement, but this is likely to lead to a well-publicised row with the school's governors, which almost every LEA understandably would wish to avoid, not least because a child's chances of successful return to a reluctant school are minimal.

Yet the 'special needs pupil' discourse creates even more serious difficulties for LEAs. Lack of clarity about criteria for assessment are compounded by lack of clarity in policies for allocating resources once needs have been identified. Children with physical disability, sensory impairment or severe learning difficulties present relatively few problems. The number of such children referred for assessment has not increased dramatically since the 1981 Act was passed. Identification of their needs can be a relatively uncontroversial matter; it is not usually difficult to agree on the nature of the children's disability, even though the educational implications may be controversial. Parents, for example, may press for support within a mainstream school while the

LEA believes the child should be placed in a special school. Mainstream placement may involve extra costs, but funding resources for these children is not what has caused LEA officers their greatest headaches.

The increase in demand for resources following the 1981 Act is attributable to the increasing number of referrals on account of learning and behavioural difficulties from Warnock's 18 per cent – in other words children who before the 1981 Act would not have been regarded as needing special educational provision. LEAs have responded to requests for support for these children in a variety of ways. The former Inner London Education Authority, abolished by the 1988 Act, set up a learning support service and allocated 0.2 of a teacher from this service to each child identified in a Statement as having learning difficulties who was to be retained in a mainstream school. While there were notable exceptions, a common pattern was for the teacher to remove the child from the class for special individual tuition for 0.2 of a week. All too often, discussion with the class teacher was minimal. For the remaining 80 per cent of the week, child and teacher had to survive as best they might. While schools were frustrated by aspects of this service, they regarded it as better than nothing, and referred pupils in increasing numbers. The increase in referrals, compounded by rate-capping, resulted in an excess of demand over supply. The ILEA responded by allocating some children 0.1 of a teacher rather than 0.2, and by putting others on a waiting list.

Other LEAs adopted *ad hoc* measures to match resources to need, but ran into similar problems. With the introduction of LMS, these were compounded by regulations that the government imposed on the amount of their overall budget which LEAs were required to delegate to schools. Three problems were emerging.

1. It was known before the 1981 Act that schools varied widely not only in the behaviour of their pupils, but also in the number of pupils they referred for specialist help (e.g. Gath *et al.*, 1977; Rutter *et al.*, 1979). The 1981 Act linked resources to a Statement of SEN, and thus provided a powerful inducement to request the formal assessment leading to a Statement. LMS provided an even more powerful inducement, as schools started to face the bleak reality of managing their own budgets. Anecdotal evidence suggests that differences between schools in referral rates remain as marked as ever, but that the overall number of referrals has increased dramatically.

2. A system which links resources to a Statement is likely to favour schools, or parents, who show the greatest determination to get the procedures completed promptly and who are most vigilant in ensuring that the resources specified in the Statement are compatible with the needs identified in professional reports. In other words, those who shout loudest get most. We found

evidence of this in our research when the intervention of an MP galvanised the LEA into action.

3. High rates of learning and behavioural problems may well reflect problems in the school's organisation, resources and teaching. This, clearly, is the implication from school effectiveness research (e.g. Rutter *et al.*, 1979; Mortimore *et al.*, 1988). The Statementing procedure, with its implicit link to the 'special needs pupil' discourse, allocates resources to the child, but this may merely legitimise the view that the problem lies with the child, and that there is no need to review the school's organisation, resources and teaching methods. Clearly, then, the 1981 and 1988 Acts have created a situation in which the largest share of resources may be allocated to the least effective schools, but allocated in a way that does little to help them become more effective.

Are there any possible solutions to this *impasse*, given the increasing determination of central government to emasculate LEAs? We have already suggested that the problem lies principally in resources for children with emotional and behavioural difficulties, and with mild or moderate learning difficulties. There should be few serious problems in finding procedures acceptable to head teachers and to parents for allocating resources for children with physical disabilities, sensory impairment, or severe learning difficulties. If taught in mainstream schools, there would be two central requirements for these children.

1. Additional resources should be allocated to the school on the child's behalf. How these resources are used should be the school's responsibility, though the school should have to account for them in the annual review of the child's Statement required by the 1981 Act and in the 4-yearly inspection cycle created by the 1991 Act. It might be inappropriate for school funding to be based on a ratio of one child with special needs counting as two 'ordinary' children or, depending on the complexity of their needs, a ratio of 1:3 or 1:4.

2. Placing responsibility on schools in this way is only realistic if teachers have access to high-quality advice and guidance from LEA support services. The critical issue here is that *teachers* should have access to this support. In other words, its function would be to help the school staff in their work with the children concerned, not to remove responsibility from teachers by providing direct tuition independently from the school.

This, however, would obviously not work for children with more general learning and behavioural difficulties. As argued above, it would penalise the most successful schools and reward the least successful. The solution here is to fund provision for special needs as generously as government regulations permit through the LMS formula. In addition, it would be essential to provide effective LEA support services as suggested for children with physical disabilities, sensory impairment and severe learning difficulties. If schools received a realistic level of SEN funding via the LMS formula, LEAs could legitimately adopt a policy of minimal Statementing. They would be able to argue that formal assessment was unnecessary on two grounds: first, the school's own informal assessment, with assistance from LEA support services, would have indicated appropriate ways to respond to the child's needs; second, the resources which a Statement would specify would already be present in the school.

Unfortunately, other legislation makes this logical approach impractical. LEAs seldom feel able to challenge decisions to exclude pupils, and, once excluded, the pupil becomes the LEA's responsibility. There is nothing in principle to prevent a LEA's LMS scheme from delegating responsibility for resources for pupils with severe behavioural problems to schools, and then charging schools when these resources are needed for pupils the school has excluded. This would enable the resources to operate on a 'user pays' basis, while allowing schools that do not use them to benefit by retaining their share of the delegated funds. The government is in fact currently considering this possibility (DFE, 1992). Again, however, the practical objections are obvious. Quite apart from the immense ill-will that this arrangement could engender, it would almost certainly encourage the already widespread practice of 'unofficial' exclusions.

An even greater difficulty is created by grant-maintained schools. LEAs have to accept responsibility for pupils excluded by those schools. They frequently have to choose between placing the child in one of their own schools, which may be understandably resentful, and using their own SEN budget to provide special resources for the rejects of grant-maintained schools.

Conclusions

The 1981 Education Act contained the seeds of its own destruction. It not only linked resources to Statements, but also extended the concept of SEN to include up to 20 per cent of children. It thus created a demand which LEAs were unable to meet and which the government had no intention of resourcing. It also aroused parental expectations which LEAs were all too often unable to fulfil. Surveying the resulting shambles, successive Secretaries of State, Micawber-like, wrung their hands and said, in effect: 'It's all the fault of the LEAs – they have to decide how to allocate resources!'

If the 1981 Act contained the seeds of its own destruction, the 1988 Education Reform Act poured rich fertiliser on to the germinating seeds. Requesting schools to compete for children ensured that they only competed for 'desirable' children. Pupils with learning and behavioural difficulties became an increasingly unwelcome commodity. Local Management of Schools required head teachers to scrutinise their budgets more closely than ever before. If a pupil needed extra resources, then these should be paid for by the LEA, and the only way to secure them was by means of a Statement. Inevitably, demand increased at precisely the same time that LEAs themselves were under greater pressure than ever before to delegate as much of their overall budget to schools as possible. Grant-maintained schools threatened the quality of LEA services to their own schools, yet LEAs had to step in and cater for pupils they excluded.

At the time of writing, the Bill which will become the 1993 Education Act was being debated in Parliament. Section III and Schedules 8–9 of this Bill revise the 1981 Act. They require that the Secretary of State:

(1) (he) shall issue, and may from time to time revise, a code of practice giving practical guidance in respect of the discharge by local education authorities of their functions under this part of the Act. . . .
(2) It shall be the duty of local education authorities discharging such functions, and of any other person exercising function for that purpose, to have regard to the provisions of the code. (Section 140)

Schedule 8 of the Bill enables the Secretary of State to issue regulations placing a duty on LEAs to complete an assessment within a specified period.

It is not yet clear what the impact will be of the new powers bestowed on the Secretary of State. They may reduce some of the seemingly interminable delays in completing assessments. That, however, may be a mixed blessing. The 1993 Act will make no changes to the funding arrangements for special educational provision, nor will it provide for any additional resources. Later in this book we shall show from our own research, and from the research of others, that the assessment process is often dominated by long and tortuous negotiations between professionals over the provision of resources. Reducing the time for their negotiation will not produce more resources. It may simply mean that bad decisions will be reached more quickly.

CHAPTER 3

The allocation and negotiation of resources

Introduction

Before the 1981 Education Act it was seldom possible to provide additional resources within a mainstream school for a child with learning difficulties. In most parts of the country, the choice lay between full-time placement in a special school or unit, and remaining full-time in the mainstream with no extra support. Educational psychologists and advisory teachers could suggest programmes that the class teacher or the school's 'remedial' teacher could apply, but some class teachers had as many as 35 children in their class, and not all schools were able to employ 'remedial' teachers. Targeting of provision combined 'hit or miss' with 'all or nothing'.

The 1981 and 1988 Acts sought to change this situation. Under the 1981 Act LEAs were required to carry out an assessment if they had reasonable grounds for thinking a child might have special educational needs. The resulting Statement could, in theory, have specified resources to be provided for the child in the mainstream school, and have had the force of law. The 1988 Act requires LEAs to include an element for special educational needs in the formula used to calculate each school's annual budget. The size of the allocation varies from LEA to LEA, depending on the amount retained centrally, but at least the principal has been established.

The special needs element in the formula is clearly intended to cater for children who do not have Statements. One might, therefore, think that fail-safe procedures had been established, *all* children with special needs being covered by one of the two Acts. Unfortunately, fail-safe procedures seldom live up to expectations. Confusion about the concept of special educational needs, and about whose responsibility it is to provide for those needs, remains as great today as before the 1981 Act, both at school level and at LEA level.

This chapter will document the conceptual confusion surrounding the purpose of assessment. Specifically, can Statements and Individual Education Programmes be reconciled with the view that special needs result from an interaction between children and their environment? We shall examine the effect of the legacy of the 1944 Act, and show how this is still reflected in the criteria which teachers use for requesting assessment. Finally, we shall examine the complex, and perhaps unexpected, effects on teachers' sense of their own professionalism of their decision to request assessment.

Statements and individualised education programmes: a case of conceptual confusion?

A central feature in Statements of special needs is that resources are targeted on the children concerned. In this respect, operation of the 1981 Act reflects the emphasis on provision of individualised education programmes, evident in the earlier United States Public Law 94/142. The 1981 Act is explicit that there is nothing absolute about the concept of special educational needs. Children's interests should be 'protected' by a Statement only if additional resources, above what the school can normally provide, are required to meet their needs. Thus a primary aged child could in theory 'need' the protection of a Statement if placed with one teacher in a mainstream school, but not if placed with a different teacher in the same school. This is by no means an uncommon situation. It does, however, raise two questions.

1. There is obvious circularity in asserting that children need a Statement (i.e. extra resources) because they need extra resources (i.e. because the school's resources are inadequate). In practice this is not a problem if we think of the school's resources in terms of equipment *and* teaching expertise. The quality and amount of equipment varies from school to school. Teacher expertise varies between schools and within them. Hence, the Statement can be seen, at least in theory, as a way of ensuring a match between the children and the resources provided for them.
2. In practice, if not in theory, the overwhelming emphasis on assessment is on the child's limitations. Reference to the school's resources, and to the ways they have helped either to meet or to create the child's problems, are usually conspicuous by their absence. This is illustrated in our own research.

We followed 29 children through each of the main stages of their assessment under the 1981 Act. Each child had been referred on account of emotional and behavioural difficulties. We analysed 26 reports from head teachers in order to identify the *principal* factors causing or contributing to the child's difficulties. At this stage we were looking for problems attributed to the child (e.g. low intelligence), to the family (e.g. tensions within the home) and to the school (e.g. inadequate resources). In Chapter 6 we report the results of a detailed content analysis of these reports, in which we take account of *all* factors mentioned. Twenty-two reports from educational psychologists were also available. In the remaining 7 cases, a decision had been made to discontinue assessment, or no report had been produced by the time we finished our fieldwork.

We also discussed with parents their belief about the principal reasons for the child's problems at school. The results are summarised in Table 3.1.

Two points should be made about these results. First, we were necessarily dealing with small numbers, as the focus of the research was an in-depth analysis of the process of assessment from the perspective of the different participants. Second, the table compares data from parents in the course of interviews with information from professional reports. At one level this is unfair. In interview some professionals were more candid about contributory factors in the school than was evident in their reports. The same was true of parents. No parent criticised the school's provision in their written response to the LEA's proposal to carry out an assessment. On the other hand, the table does indicate the gap between parents' perceptions, as reflected in what they actually say, and the formal position of teachers and educational psychologists, as reflected in their reports. The explicit professional focus on the child should be seen in the light of evidence from school effectiveness research that the school, as a social institution, and the teacher, as an individual, may have an important impact on children's learning and behaviour.

In qualifying the evidence in Table 3.1, we should also note that teachers often provided additional information in interviews with the research team to the information they felt able to include in reports seen by parents. For example, when interviewed, 16 teachers explicitly identified a child's behaviour as 'disturbed', and 14 of these explicitly attributed the disturbance to home circumstances. Interestingly, 8 teachers were explicit that the child's behaviour was not 'disturbed'.

Table 3.1 **Principal causal or contributory factors referred to in reports by head teachers and educational psychologists, and in interviews with parents**

Reference to contributory factors	Reports by head teachers (N=26)	Reports by educational psychologists (N=22)	Information from one or both Parents (N=27 children)
Child (e.g. low ability, behaviour, etc.)	18	17	10
Family	8	4	5
School	0	0	14

Some implications of research on school and teacher effectiveness

Until the late 1970s it was widely believed that children's progress and behaviour at school were determined largely, if not wholly, by constitutional factors such as intelligence and personality, and by social factors in the home and local community. The quality of their educational and social experience at school was widely assumed to have little additional influence. The Coleman Report (Coleman, *et al.*, 1966) in the United States and the Plowden Report (CACE, 1967) were associated with this view. Schools were seen as playing an important part in mitigating the effects of social disadvantage, but this was mainly through provision of additional resources, not through review and reappraisal of existing pedagogy and classroom practice.

It is now clear that this view was mistaken. When attention focuses on the process of schooling rather than on structural variables such as size and age of buildings, or organisational variables such as the organisation of pastoral care or ability grouping, a quite different picture emerges. Power *et al.*, (1972) was the first study to argue with empirical evidence that a young person's chances of appearing before the juvenile court were influenced by the school he or she attended as well as by the social environment. The teacher unions' fury at the suggestion that schools might play a part in the creation of delinquency caused an embargo on further work for several years. However, in South Wales Reynolds (1976) reported evidence that secondary modern schools exerted significantly different effects on their pupils' behaviour and educational attainments. Reynolds suggested that the more effective schools were characterised by flexibility in the way that teachers enforced school rules, particularly for older pupils.

Meanwhile, a series of studies in London led to the seminal work of Rutter *et al.* (1979). They studied 12 London secondary schools over a four year period. After taking account of pupils' social backgrounds, and of their educational attainments on entering the school, they found major differences between the 12 schools in pupils' behaviour within school, in their attendance, in their public examination results at age 16 and in their delinquency records. The differences were most marked in the case of behaviour within the school, where there was no obvious relationship with the pupils' educational attainments and social background on entry to the school. In other words, the predominant influence was that of the school. Subsequent work in London junior schools also revealed the school as a central factor in children's educational progress, and in their behaviour at school (Mortimore *et al.*, 1988) and Smith and Tomlinson (1989) also noted substantial differences between schools in their study of multiracial comprehensives. With reference to the small minority of pupils whose behaviour results in exclusion from school, Galloway *et al.*, (1982,

1985) revealed large differences between secondary schools, which could not be attributed to differences in the catchment areas they served.

The evidence, then, is clear that schools exert an important influence on children's behaviour and on their educational progress. The obvious inference is that whether children develop learning or behavioural difficulties requiring assessment under the 1981 Act may depend at least in part on the school they happen to be attending. This would be true even if criteria for requesting assessment were objective and uncontroversial – for example, a reading age more than two years below chronological age, or more than two years below the level predicted by IQ, or certain measurable behaviour patterns. In reality, criteria for assessment are neither objective nor uncontroversial. The objective differences between schools in their influence on children's behaviour and progress are compounded by the subjective nature of teachers' assessments that children's special needs may require additional resources.

The research summarised above appears at first sight to support the 'school and teacher effectiveness' discourse of special educational needs (see p.15). In theory the current funding arrangements are compatible with the consequent implications. The special needs element in the financial formula for local management of schools can be used for professional development purposes, to improve the quality of teaching and resources for vulnerable pupils. In practice, a different picture emerges. Having children with learning and/or behaviour problems in their class increases teachers' feeling of stress (Galloway *et al.*, 1987).

High stress and low job satisfaction do not encourage people to evaluate their current practice, since they recognise all too clearly that the evaluation may itself create further stress. The effect of high stress and low job satisfaction is rather to increase a tendency to rely on the 'special needs pupil' discourse. In other words, the problem is seen as residing 'in' the child, rather than in the interaction between child and school or classroom environment. In pointing out that this implicitly denies the school's possible contribution to the problem, we should not overlook the fact that it is self-protective. It goes some way towards protecting teachers from feelings of failure, and, as we shall see shortly, enables them to assert their expertise in teaching 'ordinary' children.

While it might be true to assert that the 1981 Act actively encourages teachers to resort to the 'special needs pupil' discourse, it would also be an oversimplification. Clearly, resources are linked to Statements. However, we also need to consider the historical legacy on which the 1981 Act was based, and to explore the consequent culturally based assumptions about the school system's function *vis-à-vis* the individual and society.

The historical legacy: social control and the cult of individualism

By creating categories of handicap, and by requiring LEAs to provide special educational 'treatment' for children ascertained as 'suffering' from one of the handicaps, the 1944 Education Act established parallel systems of mainstream and special education. Relatively few teachers, or children, transferred from special schools to the mainstream. DES (1975) guidelines made transfer into special schools, and out of them, easier to arrange on an informal basis than had previously been the case, and easier than is the case under the 1981 Act. Nevertheless, the separateness of the special school system remained firmly established. The physical separation of special schools was reflected not only in a more limited curriculum but also in a similarly parallel structure within the LEA's central administration. Typically, one assistant education officer would have responsibility for special schools, and another for mainstream schools. Similarly, advisers or inspectors were appointed either to the mainstream or to the special sector.

These structural divisions encouraged territorial behaviour, thus deepening the divide. Professionals in the special sector established their territory and tried to expand it. When David Galloway joined a LEA schools psychology service in 1972, educational psychologists were actively encouraged by personnel in the central administration to refer more pupils to schools for children labelled ESN-M (educationally subnormal, moderate) or maladjusted than the schools could actually cater for; long waiting lists could be used as a lever to persuade the Education Committee to expand this sector. It sometimes led to bizarre demarcation disputes. Maladjusted children were part of the 'special' territory. On the other hand, 'disruptives' were part of the mainstream territory. The reason was partly that it was administratively easier to open units or centres for disruptive pupils than special schools. Indeed, provided the pupil remained on the roll of a mainstream school with the theoretical possibility of returning, units could be opened with minimal formality. An additional reason, however, was that admission to units could often be arranged more quickly than to special schools. Hence, mainstream education officers soon regarded units as an important resource for responding to pressure from head teachers to 'do something' about a pupil.

Although administratively often separate from special schools, the explosion in off-site provision for disruptive pupils in the 1970s and 1980s did nothing to reduce the division between the mainstream and various forms of special provision. To understand the underlying reasons for this division we need to examine two related issues, each of which has had a profound impact on the culture of teaching as a profession. The first concerns conflicting perspectives on the purpose of special educational provision, and the second, the essentially individualistic ethos which has characterised schools in recent years.

Benevolent humanitarianism or social control?

A conventional view sees special provision as a humanitarian response to needs that would not otherwise be met. Recommendations for special school placement are, after all, invariably couched in language which emphasises its benefits for the child. A more critical view sees special provision as a form of social control, whereby teachers can secure the removal of troublesome and slow-learning children from their classrooms (e.g. Tomlinson, 1981a and b, 1982).

The social control argument can be applied to all children in special schools, irrespective of the nature and severity of their learning difficulties. It is concerned both with curriculum and with behaviour management. In some states of Canada, children with severe and multiple disabilities are integrated into mainstream classes (Shaw, 1990). With current funding levels it is hard to envisage this in Britain, although there is evidence that young children with Down's syndrome may make better progress in mainstream than in special schools (Casey *et al.*, 1988). Successful integration involves the twin challenges of adjusting the curriculum for the child concerned without reducing the quality of learning for the majority. It often requires specialist teaching, ancillary support and ready access to para-medical services such as speech, physio- and occupational therapy. In Britain neither LEAs nor district health authorities give priority to this level of resourcing. Without it, mainstream teachers can legitimately insist on children's removal to special schools or classes on the grounds: (a) that they cannot cope with the curriculum requirements; (b) that if they were to try, the education of other children would suffer.

The much larger number of children with less severe, or 'moderate' learning difficulties, and emotional and behavioural difficulties, raise additional questions. These children are more likely to present an overt challenge to the authority of teachers and to their competence. The special needs of those children are usually identified for the first time at school. Their parents and relatives often regard them as 'normal': perhaps a bit 'slow', perhaps 'difficult' but nevertheless 'normal'. Overwhelmingly, they come from working-class backgrounds, unlike children with severe learning difficulties, physical disabilities and sensory impairment, for whom there is a relatively even social class distribution. In other words, teacher assessment that they have special educational needs is based on a normative judgement of what constitutes acceptable progress and behaviour.

The widespread belief that children who present learning and behavioural problems are increasingly being integrated into the mainstream has little basis in fact. Indeed, some evidence suggests an increase in separate provision for primary-aged children (Swann, 1985). Moreover, frequent press reports have noted an increase in indefinite exclusion and expulsions from school. This is not surprising in view of the wider context in which schools are working.

Until the mid-1970s unemployment levels were low. Almost all school-leavers could expect a job, irrespective of their qualifications. A substantial minority of pupils were simply contained in school; they derived little educational benefit, frequently became disaffected, and frequently truanted, but no one talked about them as having special educational needs or needing alternative provision. In the early 1970s they were known as the ROSLA pupils – the pupils who would have left school at 15 before the raising of the school leaving age to 16.

Today the position has changed. High unemployment rates, parents with higher educational aspirations for their children, and a legal requirement that schools publish their exam results have all combined to ensure that pupils who would once have been quietly contained are now regarded as serious educational and management problems. The National Curriculum is a legal requirement for these pupils. They cannot now be offered a simplified curriculum designed, ostensibly, for their limited abilities. Further, schools are now competing for pupils, and pupils who fail to reach the required standard, or to behave in approved ways, are a threat to the school's public image. Special educational needs may have been given a higher profile by the attention of HMI, by the 1981 Act and by the formula for local management of schools, but the net result of economic and legislative changes of the 1980s has been to increase pressures on mainstream pupils who, for one reason or another, do not conform.

There is nevertheless one sense in which the perspectives of benevolent humanitarianism and social control may not be incompatible. The social control argument is concerned essentially with the function of provision for special educational needs within the education system, whether in special or in mainstream schools. It is not concerned with the motivation of individuals within that system. Many individuals within the system may have been motivated by altruism. Thus, many special school teachers derive their job satisfaction from knowledge that the pupils with whom they feel they are working successfully have failed in the mainstream, and have been failed by it. Similarly SEN specialists in the mainstream often see themselves as compensating for the limitations of children's learning experiences in ordinary classes. Mainstream class and subject teachers, too, may assert with complete integrity that they recognise the limitation in what they can offer, and are concerned both about a particular individual and about the impact of this individual on the rest of the class. Not infrequently, other evidence seems to contradict the assertion of altruism. Some special schools, for example, have low expectations and offer an unstimulating curriculum; some mainstream teachers belittle children with learning or behavioural problems. That, however, is not the point. Arguing that the function of provision for special educational needs is to make teaching easier in the mainstream, and either to remove misfits or to socialise them into conformity, does not invalidate the argument that individuals may be motivated by what sociologists call benevolent humanitarianism.

The cult of individualism

Hargreaves (1982) argued that the secondary school system was failing a large minority of its pupils. It is clear that the pupils to whom Hargreaves was referring include most of those whom Warnock described as having special educational needs and Joseph as the 'bottom 40 per cent'. Hargreaves attributed the failure of the education system with so many pupils to the 'cult' of individualism. Schools, he argued, have become so involved with concern about the rights, progress and welfare of the individual that they have lost sight of corporate aspects of school life. Personal identity is established in a social context, and if this social context fails to provide a sense of belonging, young people may find it for themselves through membership of peer groups which consciously reject the school's aims and values. In its most extreme form, this is seen in the groups of disaffected low-achieving or under-achieving teenagers in years 10 and 11. In a less extreme form it is seen in many younger children who rely for social approval from other pupils on behaviour which their teachers dismiss as 'silly' or 'attention-seeking'.

Extending Hargreaves' argument, the cult of individualism is evident in the rhetoric of special educational needs. There is much talk of *individual* needs, *individual* educational programmes, *individualised* learning. We hear much less about programmes which see the individual as a socially active and contributing member of the school community. Yet there is ample evidence about the social consequences of being identified as having special educational needs. Simmons (1986) has described the embarrassment pupils can feel when withdrawn from ordinary classes. At conference and in-service workshops on special needs, it seldom takes more than 5 minutes for teachers to produce a list of more than 50 derogatory names which mainstream pupils use to describe their contemporaries with special needs. These have ranged from the ubiquitous 'spas' to 'remmo', presumably a corruption of 'remedial', to 'bum-boys' from the alleged sexual orientation of the teacher in charge. Yet although the social consequences of identification cannot seriously be doubted, we continue to rely on the rhetoric of meeting *individual* needs. This obvious anomaly only starts to make sense when we examine the criteria teachers use for requesting assessment, and the 'hidden' purposes of assessment from their perspective.

Teachers' criteria for assessment: an empirical study

Disturbed or disruptive?

When requesting formal assessment under the 1981 Act, many teachers in our study implicitly drew a distinction between 'disturbed' and 'disruptive' behaviour. This implies a qualitative difference, yet Graham and Rutter (1970) have claimed that children's psychiatric disorders should not be seen as diseases or illnesses, and that the behaviour of children 'diagnosed' as having psychiatric disorder will not differ qualitatively from that of other children. This is consistent with the philosophy of the 1981 Act, which explicitly rejects a definition of SEN in terms of medical or quasi-medical categories. 'Psychiatric disorder' and 'emotional disturbance' can be seen as examples of such categories. Section 1(i) of the Act defines children as having SEN when they have a learning difficulty which calls for special educational provision over and above that normally available in a mainstream school. Galloway and Goodwin (1987, p.32) summarise their review of work in this area:

> The common point to emerge from medical and psychological attempts to classify behaviour disorders or describe types of maladjustment is that at best maladjustment is a rag-tag term for describing any behaviour which teachers, psychologists or doctors find disturbing.

Yet in spite of its theoretical and empirical weakness, teachers of 16 of the 29 children involved saw this distinction between 'disruptive' and 'disturbed' as important. Their views are evident in the Elton Report on discipline in schools (DES, 1989b). This claims that children have emotional and behavioural difficulties when they show

> ... severe and persistent behaviour problems as a result of emotional, psychological or neurological disturbance so that their needs cannot be met in mainstream schools. (Para. 6–29)

The rather obvious circularity in this definition is not helped by the report's suggestion that relevant professionals should decide when it applies. Nevertheless, the basis of the distinction between 'disruptive' and 'disturbed', drawn by teachers of over half the children in the sample, lay in their perception of the child's ability to control his or her own behaviour. Quotations from teachers illustrate this point:

> He's just crackers, absolutely crackers. He talks to himself and answers himself back. He walks around the school making weird physical gestures . . . . psychologically the kid is disturbed. He needs help.

> I've got a very bad class this year – a lot of difficult boys. But Damien isn't like them. With them it's because they get no discipline. With Damien that's not it. He's just strange.

Origins of EBD

When interviewed, teachers in 14 of these 16 cases identified the origins of the child's emotional and behavioural difficulties as home circumstances. One head, for example, described a child as having:

a crazy home background with little or no control over him . . . his behaviour outbursts are manifestations of an emotionally disturbed youngster.

In a further 8 cases the children's behaviour problems at school were attributed mainly to family factors, even though there was no reference to their being 'emotionally disturbed'. One teacher wrote:

Whilst the school may respond to school-based interventions to curb his outbursts, there does not seem to be any noticeable improvement in his behaviour at home. It may, therefore, be that a mainstream school is not a suitable setting for Michael's education.

The common theme in all these cases was a reference to factors over which teachers felt they had no control. This had important consequences for what they expected the assessment to achieve. In theory, a major function of assessment is to determine whether or not the child has special educational needs. That, however, had already been decided, at least by the head teacher when referring the child. Invariably, they had much more specific expectations regarding the outcome of assessments. These expectations were expressed in terms of the school's needs as well as those of the child concerned. From the psychologist's perspective, the problem did not lie principally in making a clinical judgement about the child, but rather in negotiating a solution that would be acceptable to all parties.

The psychologist's room to manoeuvre could, however, be severely restricted. Seventeen of the 29 children were excluded from school either before their assessment started or while it was in progress. Except in the cases of the minority of temporary exclusions, this left educational psychologists very limited room to manoeuvre. If the exclusion was indefinite or permanent, they could, in theory, describe the child's needs in terms of a return to the same mainstream school or to a different one. In practice, there were two obstacles to this. First, the governors would be almost certain to support the head teacher's decision to exclude the pupil. Moreover, the local grapevine normally ensured that no neighbouring school would willingly accept the child. Second, and more important, recommendations of this sort would place psychologists in direct conflict with head teachers, and the success of any future work in the school would depend on maintaining good relationships with heads. Yet even if the exclusion was only temporary, it very clearly had the effect of increasing pressures on the psychologist to propose a solution that the school would find acceptable. Without such a solution, the threat of indefinite or permanent exclusion would continue to hang over the child – *and* over the psychologist!

The purpose of assessment: teacher perspectives

At one level the purpose of assessment is obvious; to provide appropriate help for a child with special needs. Yet as the cases of the 17 pupils in our study who were excluded from school make clear the underlying purpose is seldom so straightforward. As part of our research, we investigated the effect of assessment on teacher's perceptions of their own professional role. In our analysis we drew on sociological research (e.g. Apple, 1982; Ozga and Lawn, 1981) and in particular on the usefulness of the concepts of 'de-skilling' and 'proletarianisation'. Lawn and Ozga (1988) have argued that structural changes in society have led to the 'proletarianisation' of teachers, the main features of which include the loss of traditional classroom skills and knowledge, loss of autonomy within the classroom, an increase in feelings of stress, an increase in supervision at middle management or senior management levels, and the development of new skilled specialisations. In the present context, these new specialisations would include responsibility for pastoral care and special needs within the school, and psychological and advisory services outside it. Lawn and Ozga argue that attempts by people outside the teaching profession to specify the skills of teaching – or, for our present purposes, managing children with behaviour problems – challenge the professional autonomy of teachers; thereby, they serve to control and de-skill the teacher's work.

We have already argued that assessment is requested on account of emotional and behavioural difficulties when teachers feel that the child's behaviour:

(a) is 'disturbed', and different in some qualitative way from more readily understood 'disruptive' behaviour;
(b) results from a difficult home background over which the school has no control.

This is consistent with the view that requests for formal assessment illustrate the process by which teachers become de-skilled or proletarianised: outside experts are invited, at least implicitly, to accept responsibility for the problem, and to advise on future action. Teachers, however, negotiate from a stronger position than is often realised. From their perspective, it may be the educational psychologist who is de-skilled.

It was common for teachers, when interviewed, to argue that on a one-to-one basis (as they maintained, incorrectly, would be the case in schools specialising in the teaching of children with emotional and behavioural difficulties) they could easily cope with the emotionally disturbed child. Teachers asserted that such children could not be taught within the normal classroom context, not because of a lack of skill on their part but rather because the needs of these children impeded the educational progress of other children in the same class. The nature of this process by which a child's needs are negotiated between professionals in terms of a parallel negotiation of their roles can be seen in the case of Bryan, which we shall discuss in greater detail in Chapter 9.

In Bryan's case the psychologist realised that the head teacher 'might have been laying it on a bit heavy by demanding a special school for Bryan so as to force my hand to give her what she really wanted'. The outcome was that Bryan remained in the mainstream school, as the educational psychologist preferred, but the school received additional resources. The school saw the psychologist as gatekeeper to these resources. More important, teachers saw his professional role as arranging access to them rather than as provider of clinical or educational advice about the child's needs. At this stage, therefore, the school was relying on his administrative ability, not on his expertise as a clinician or as an expert in special educational needs. What was more important, though, was the implication that extra resources were needed to cater for a 'disturbed' child like Bryan. By defining their own professional skills in terms of their expertise in teaching 'ordinary' children, teachers could demand extra resources for teaching Bryan.

Conclusions

In negotiating the nature of a child's needs and how they should be met, some participants are clearly more powerful than others. The inequality of power between professionals and parents (Swann, 1987; Tomlinson, 1981a; Wood, 1988) and between parents and children (Armstrong *et al.*, in press) may be contrasted with the rhetoric of equality which professionals frequently adopt in their negotiations with each other (Armstrong *et al.*, 1991). These latter negotiations are based on the assumption that each party has an essential contribution to make, and thus has more or less equal power to influence events. Yet teacher perceptions of the psychologist's role can influence the agenda in the assessment process. This was seen in Bryan's assessment when his teachers' perceptions of their own needs significantly affected the outcome of the psychologist's assessment, even though, in the latter's expert judgement, there was good reason to doubt the need for a Statement.

Far from de-skilling teachers, their negotiations led them to adopt strategies which secured acceptable outcomes – notably, defining their own role in a way that not only asserted their own expertise with ordinary children, but also limited the psychologist's role.

The theoretical simplicity of current policies for resourcing special needs provision must be compared with the complexity of the interpersonal and micro-political processes in practice. In theory, Statements protect the interest of children whose needs require more resources than a mainstream school can normally supply. The allocation for special needs in the school's annual budget under local management of schools should ensure adequate provision for the majority of the 20 per cent of pupils regarded by the Warnock Committee as having special educational needs (DES, 1978). The reality is that as teachers struggle to implement the National Curriculum, they have become increasingly alarmed by the presence of slow-learning or 'disturbed' children, and recognise the implications of schools competing with each other for pupils in a market-oriented education system. At the same time, LEAs have been stripped of many of their historical powers, and have been required to fund resources for an ever-increasing number of children for whom statements are requested within static or declining budgets. In Part II we shall examine the process of assessment in this increasingly difficult climate from the perspectives of children, parents and professionals.

PART II

Children's, parents' and professional perspectives

CHAPTER 4

Children's perspectives on assessment

Introduction

Much has been written on the topic of children with special educational needs, yet little is known about how children perceive their own needs or about their understanding of how these needs are assessed. In this chapter we examine the very significant changes that are taking place in child care legislation and practice. We contrast these with the position of children in the education system and discuss the relevance of debates on children's rights to participate in decision-making for children whose special educational needs are being assessed. Using case study data from our research on the assessment of children identified as having emotional and behavioural difficulties, we show how children's perceptions of professionals – i.e. their metaperceptions – can affect their behaviour in ways that professionals might not recognise. Finally, we consider some of the constraints on professionals' ability to gain access to the child's perspective.

Background

The popular notion that 'children should be seen and not heard' once dominated every aspect of the child's relationships with adults in positions of authority. This principal was applied in matters relating to children's health, to their care and control in the family and to their education. Children were not only powerless, they rarely had even the right to be consulted or listened to by adults making decisions on their behalf. Denied the status of participants in the social system they were often reduced to being seen as the property of their parents (Freeman, 1987).

The development of child-centred educational philosophies, particularly following the publication of the Plowden Report (CACE, 1967), represented a major challenge to traditional perceptions of the *value* of children. Yet, such challenges were themselves, perhaps necessarily, premised upon adult preconceptions of children's interests. As such they raised complex and frequently perplexing problems concerning the relationship between adult responsibilities and children's rights. Some of these, such as the William Tyndale experiment (ILEA, 1976) grabbed the headlines, while others, attempting to derive a theory of children's rights from philosophical principles, have had only a marginal effect on public policy and public perceptions of children in society (King, 1981; Wringe, 1973).

Public perceptions of the vulnerability of children, and of their right to be heard, have perhaps been more significantly changed by the often harrowing disclosures of child abuse and maltreatment within both families and child care institutions that began to emerge in the 1970s and 1980s. Moreover, as evidence of child abuse increasingly came to public attention taboos inhibiting its discussion began to fall away. As this happened, more and more adults, who themselves had been the victims of abuse when children, felt able to talk about their experiences (Allen, 1980; Armstrong, 1978; Brady, 1979; Ward, 1984). This combination of personal revelation and public scandal has had far-reaching effects on social work practice in particular. Pressure has mounted both within and from outside social services departments for children's views to be taken seriously (Gardner, 1985, 1987), though the response to this has not been uniform.

The Cleveland scandal and the subsequent inquiry into procedures for identifying and dealing with cases of child abuse (Butler-Sloss, 1988) probably did more to awaken public awareness in this area than any case that preceded it. Yet this was a case that highlighted the pitfalls faced by professionals in their attempts to act in the interests of children. Significantly the report of the inquiry into this case recommended that professionals should always listen carefully to children and take what they say seriously, maintaining that

the views and wishes of the child, particularly as to what should happen to him/her, should be taken into account by the professionals involved with their problems. (Butler-Sloss, 1988, p. 245)

Running parallel to these developments, the appeal court's judgement in the case of Gillick (1986) had major implications for the legal rights of children. In this case the appeal court decided that where a girl had the maturity and understanding to evaluate different courses of action she could seek and be given contraceptive advice without the permission of her parents. This case was widely seen as implying that where a child had the maturity to make decisions about contraception she also had the maturity to make decisions in many other areas of her life (Freeman, 1987).

The 1989 Children Act

The climate of concern over the vulnerability of children where control over their lives is placed entirely in the hands of adults is centrally reflected in the 1989 Children Act. This legislation, for the first time, placed a statutory duty on those with responsibility for identifying children's needs to take account of

the ascertainable wishes and feelings of the child concerned (considered in the light of his age and understanding). (Section 1(3))

This legislation is likely to have consequences reaching far beyond those matters falling within the direct jurisdiction of the courts. Decision-making about children's special educational needs and the allocation of resources are areas that are likely to be affected (Cross and Gallagher, 1991). However, at the present time it is difficult to gauge the precise implications of the legislation in this area.

Davies (1991) has suggested that the viability of residential special schools may be undermined by the requirement in the Act for local authorities to take seriously children's requests for placement in institutions within the same locality as their families. White *et al.* (1990) point out that, where an assessment of a child is ordered by the court, Section 44(7) of the Act gives the child the right

if he is of sufficient understanding to make an informed decision (to) refuse to submit to the examination or other assessment. (p. 106)

This may be contrasted with the legal duty the 1981 Education Act places on parents to present their child for medical assessment.

Although the 1989 Children Act might be seen as introducing a radical extension of children's rights, a cautionary note has been sounded by the Children's Legal Centre (Childright, 1991) who have drawn attention to anomalies in the Act. These, it points out, mean that the Act only safeguards children in three institutions (local authority children's homes, private 'registered' children's homes and independent schools taking less than 50 children). Parry-Jones (1991) has gone further, questioning the ability of children covered by the Act to exercise their new found rights. He argues that this is seriously impeded by the absence of a corresponding right to information. Without such a right it is difficult to see how children can form an opinion about whether or not they should exercise their rights in any particular situation. These and other anomalies are only likely to be resolved as a body of case law is built up in the courts.

Children's perspectives on education

Concern over the rights of children has principally focused on those who have suffered abuse, maltreatment and neglect at the hands of adults. This concern has not significantly affected the status of children's views in situations where adults do not judge them to have the same vulnerability. Children have very few 'rights' in respect of decisions made about them, including decisions about their education (Rosenbaum and Newell, 1991).

Fundamental changes in the British education system introduced in the 1980s were premised upon a philosophy of consumer choice (White, 1988). The power of professionals to be arbiters of the legitimate aims and methods of education was brought into question as attempts were made to make schools and teachers accountable to the 'market'. Parents were given new rights of choice, of access to information about their children's education, and of control through participation in the management of schools. Yet, at no time were children's views sought about the changes to be introduced. Moreover, it was parents and future employers who were identified as the consumers of education, not children. Children cannot, for instance, be represented on the governing bodies of schools, nor do they have any right to be consulted about changes in school policy. By failing to provide children with the right to be consulted regarding decisions affecting their interests the 1986 Education Act and the 1988 Education Reform Act sit awkwardly with the general thrust of child care legislation and practice in recent years.

In this respect the 1988 Act may undermine the innovative work of those educational professionals who have argued in favour of children being given a greater say in their own learning. For instance, the development of records of achievement and pupil profiling (Broadfoot, 1986) appear to have been ignored despite recent theoretical and empirical work on classroom learning which indicates that children make sense of their learning experiences through their actions as decision-makers (e.g. Nisbet and Schucksmith, 1986).

Further support for the view that children should be listened to comes from the research of psychologists investigating children's motivational styles. Little (1985), for example, has demonstrated the importance of children's beliefs about the way others perceive them. The complexity of the interaction, Little argues, can only be understood by examining the categories and attributions that children use in their accounts of their beliefs and actions. Conceptual systems imposed on children's beliefs by adults are likely to lead to a distortion of the intended meanings. Similarly, it might be argued that adults' perceptions of children's beliefs and interests will be inadequate and even false where no attempt is made to explore these from the child's own perspective. Assumptions made by adults about children's behaviour may lead to the rationality of children's own accounts of their behaviour being questioned. This can lead to children's views being disregarded 'in their own interests'. Thus assumptions about rationality, based upon adults' preconceptions of rational behaviour, may cause children to be disempowered. By contrast, research in North America has shown that programmes aimed at preventing the emergence of behavioural and psychological problems in schools can be successfully implemented where children are treated as rational agents making rational responses to situations that may be anything but rational (Bond and Compas, 1989; Trueba *et al.*, 1989).

Research that has attempted to gain access to the perspectives of 'difficult' children is nonetheless rare. Some exceptions to this do stand out. In particular a number of well-known school ethnographies carried out in the 1960s and 1970s contributed to our understanding of children's educational experiences (Hargreaves, 1967; Hargreaves *et al.*, 1975; Willis, 1977; Woods, 1979). Despite these studies, Barton and Meighan (1979) concluded that the pupil's perspective was one of the most under-researched areas in education. That remains the case today. During the 1980s, interest in children's perspectives declined substantially. One reason for this has been suggested by Giroux (1983, p. 43):

In the face of financial cutbacks, economic recession and a shrinking job market progressive and radical critiques of schooling . . . have given way to the logic of instrumental reason, with its directed focus on the learning of discrete competencies and basic skills.

The 1981 Education Act

The concept of 'partnership' is as central to the 1981 Education Act as it was to the Warnock Report (DES, 1978) that preceded it. Interprofessional partnership and parent–professional partnership are recurring themes in recent thinking on special education, yet the 1981 Act says nothing about the child's contribution to the assessment process. In this respect it is clearly located in the pre-Gillick era when the possibility of conflict between the interests of children and their parents was not fully recognized.

Although lacking any legal basis in the legislation itself, the Department of Education and Science (DES, 1983, 1989a) has nonetheless attempted to define 'good practice' in this area to take account of current thinking on children's rights. Thus, in its circular 22/89 it advises that:

The feelings and perceptions of the child should be taken into account and the concept of partnership should whenever possible be extended to older children and young persons. (DES, 1989a, para. 21)

However, translating these 'good intentions' into procedures for ensuring the involvement of children in decision-making is far from straightforward. The lack of any formal procedures for giving children the right to be consulted and be involved in decision-making about the nature of their special educational needs (indeed, whether or not the need is theirs at all!) means that in practice they are often assigned a passive role. Gersch (1987, p. 154) describes the conventional role allotted to the child in the assessment process as follows:

Although the process and purpose of assessment may vary from professional to professional, and indeed there are different emphases on tests, observation and other techniques, children themselves are conventionally ascribed a subservient role in the whole assessment process. They are often expected to carry out specified tasks, answer specific questions, undertake written activities or follow set procedures. The child is generally seen as a relatively 'passive object', and assessment is viewed as something which is 'done to the child' rather than involving the child very actively.

In Chapter 6 we describe in more detail the range of measures used by psychologists when carrying out their assessments of the children in our study. However, it is clear from this evidence that, despite their awareness of the DES advice and support for it in principle, educational psychologists rarely adopted procedures for gaining access to the child's point of view. Most interviews with children focused upon psychometric measures of 'ability', 'intelligence' and, more rarely, 'personality disorders'.

Children's perceptions of the assessment process

Evidence from our own research suggests that the lack of involvement children have in the decision-making process is reflected in their ignorance about how decisions are reached. This could lead to children having serious misperceptions about the purpose of the assessment and about the role of professionals taking part in it. Retrospective interviews with 18 children attending two residential schools and one off-site unit for disruptive children revealed that only 3 children were able to offer an account of the psychologist's role in their assessment. For one child, beliefs about the role of the psychologist served to reinforce his sense of personal deficit. The psychologist wanted to 'find out what was wrong with me'.

An interview with another child illustrated the confusion many children in this sample felt about the role of the professionals they had seen:

I had to see him because of my temper tantrums. I used to be a bit of a psycho. The psychologist talked to me to calm me down. . . . The psychologist felt my backbone all the way up and said it was crooked. I don't know why they were doing this.

Another child said of the medical assessment:

I had a brain scan. This thing on my head with lots of wires to see if there was owt wrong with me, if I was dyslexic or what. I don't know what they said about it.

Children in the sample reported how their anxieties about the assessment were fuelled by a lack of information about its purpose. If these children are to be believed it seems they had little more than their own assumptions and the beliefs, or threats of their parents, to guide them in interpreting events. Joanne, for example, said that she had been worried by the prospect of a meeting with a psychologist:

I didn't like the thought of it. My mum used to call him a 'brain shrink'. I don't know why but it made me a bit suspicious. It made me feel something was wrong with me. My mum said if you saw a brain shrink there's something wrong with your head. I used to knock my head to make sure there was nothing wrong and it was still working.

A similar anxiety was reported by Susan after she was asked to attend for a medical examination as part of the assessment:

I was dreading going. I don't know why. I was nervous and dreading going.

In both these cases the children felt that they had been left to make their own sense of their interviews with psychologists and doctors. Joanne said that after being interviewed by the psychologist

I went back home and told my mum he wasn't a brain shrink because he didn't ask me about my brain.

Susan, commenting on the doctor's assessment, said

I don't think she found anything wrong with me but she never told me.

Although these accounts offer an interesting insight into the way children perceive the assessment process there are methodological problems in establishing the veracity of the claims made when the sole source of information is a retrospective interview. Children's memories of the assessment may have become blurred. Alternatively, information might have been given to them by the professionals but this information may have been misunderstood by the children. The methodology we adopted in the main part of this study, however, enabled us to overcome this problem. Our observation of the key parts of the assessment in the cases of 29 children, including psychologists' interviews with those children, gave us the opportunity to contrast participant's accounts of their experience of the assessment with our own record of those events.

It was clear from these observations that the psychologists in our study found difficulty in pitching their explanations of the assessment at a level that made sense to the children. Most psychologists did explain something about the procedures to the children, but from the child's perspective the decision to initiate the assessment was frequently interpreted as subordinating their own account to that of those who had requested the assessment – usually teachers, but occasionally parents. For the most part, the children in this sample identified aspects of their own behaviour as probably unacceptable to others. Nevertheless, they contended that the difficult behaviour they presented had its origin in more complex problems, often related directly to their experience in school. When children saw outside professionals responding to teachers' or parents' perceptions of the 'problem', they tended to regard their assessment as part of a punishment they had been given. Nineteen of the children explicitly referred to the assessment in these terms.

Darren, for instance, was one child who believed the assessment was taking place because his teachers were 'saying I was the worst 1st year'.

In discussing the circumstances of his case with a researcher, Darren contrasted his teachers' views with his own account of the problems he faced in secondary school:

There were a lot of people aggravating me because I wasn't bright. I was more or less the thickest kid in the class and I used to smash out at them. . . . I got on with the teachers bad. They just didn't know what my problems were. . . . I used to always get taken the rip out of and that was the trouble really. I never bothered to listen. I just sat there making jokes.

When seen by the psychologist, however, Darren made no reference to his feelings about the way the situation had deteriorated in school *even though the psychologist had tried to give him the opportunity to make his views known.* Far from the assessment providing him with a genuine opportunity to put his side of the story and have it given equal consideration, Darren saw his referral to the psychologist as an expression of the power the school had over him and a means through which its view of the world could be enforced:

There was nothing I could say really because they wouldn't have me back in school. . . . I didn't want to be away from my family and friends but he (the psychologist) put me here (residential school). He's the one who got me sent away.

Darren believed there was nothing he could contribute to the assessment because he had no control over the issues that had been identified as important or over the decisions that were ultimately going to be made about his future.

The way the referral of a child operates to disempower the child can also be seen in David's assessment. David was 12 years old when referred by his teachers to the schools' psychological service. The referral was made by his teachers in response to his parents' concerns about his behaviour. Yet our methodology enables us to maintain with some confidence that David's parents received no adequate explanation about the purpose or meaning of the assessment procedures. Nor, in this case, was any explanation of the purpose of the assessment given by the psychologist to David. After his parents received a letter from the LEA informing them that he was to be assessed in accordance with Section 5 of the 1981 Education Act, David believed this meant he was to be 'sectioned' under mental health legislation and that he would be admitted to a psychiatric hospital. This interpretation fitted with his parents' beliefs about his mental state. They maintained throughout that there was 'something wrong in his head' and David had in fact been seen by a psychiatrist on a previous occasion at their request, though nothing had come of this. The lack of detailed explanation and discussion about the different stages of the assessment of David's special educational needs served, in this case, to reinforce his parents' misconceptions about its purpose. In turn these misconceptions legitimated his parents' beliefs and enabled them to shift responsibility for his difficulties away from themselves and on to David's shoulders. Thus, by focusing attention upon David rather than upon the relationships within his family, the assessment, unintentionally, added to the problems David was encountering. The lack of information available to him impeded his ability to make sense of the assessment other than in terms of his own personal deficit. Yet, because this was his understanding of the purpose of the assessment, he was unable to contribute anything to it.

Children's metaperceptions of the assessment

There was evidence in at least 20 cases in our research sample of children's beliefs about the purpose of the assessment and the role of the professionals (i.e., the children's metaperceptions) having an effect upon the child's behaviour during the assessment. In one of these, Stephen's psychologist was recommending a placement in a residential school – a recommendation which was opposed by Stephen's parents. His parents attempted to thwart this outcome by transferring Stephen to a new mainstream primary school. Up to that point reports of Stephen's behaviour had indicated a steady deterioration, but once he had changed schools and the assessment had been suspended to 'give him a chance to fail', Stephen commented,

now I can start being good.

This outcome allowed him, in his own view, the opportunity to reassert control over his behaviour and act according to the changed expectations people had of him. According to the teachers at the new school, his transfer was reasonably smooth, and the assessment was subsequently abandoned.

Where professionals have been unable to gain access to the child's perspective they may misinterpret the child's behaviour during the assessment. Yet it is reasonable to assume that the recommendations they make will be influenced by the behaviour they encounter from the child during the assessment. The implications for a child of a breakdown in communication of this sort may be serious. This may be illustrated by looking at Peter's assessment.

Peter was referred directly to the educational psychologist when he was in his last year of primary schooling. In an assessment of Peter his psychologist used a range of personality measures. These suggested that Peter was showing signs of a personality disorder. In a subsequent interview with Peter the psychologist noted that he presented as 'uncooperative' and 'unemotional'. This behaviour, according to the psychologist, was confirmation of his hypothesis:

He's very introverted with a high level of neuroticism and a range of features that indicate he is specifically depressed – a reduction of interest – one could almost say he showed no emotion.

This view was supported by the clinical medical officer (CMO) who carried out a medical assessment of Peter as part of the Statementing procedures. In a discussion with the educational psychologist the CMO commented:

He didn't display any emotion about his life. Nothing seemed to surprise him about his home and social life.

These observations were used by the psychologist and CMO in support of their joint recommendation that Peter would benefit from placement in a residential school for children with emotional and behavioural difficulties.

In a later interview with Peter the psychologist reiterated his view that it would be best for him if he went to a residential school:

You know I'm thinking of an entirely different sort of school for you. A residential school where you don't come home until the holidays. What do you think about that?

Peter's response was an emphatic 'no' but when asked by the psychologist to elaborate upon this he remained silent. This silence could clearly be interpreted in different ways, one of which was advanced by the psychologist, i.e. a personality disorder. However, the child's own account of these interviews, given in a subsequent discussion with a researcher, suggested a different interpretation from that chosen by the psychologist. From Peter's own perspective the assessment threatened his chances of continuing to live with his family and as such was a source of considerable anxiety:

The psychologist wants to send me away . . . they're horrible there (residential schools). You get put in strait-jackets if you're naughty. You get locked up and they have walls round to keep you in.

For Peter this anxiety about the role of the psychologist led him to distrust the psychologist's intentions and hence led to his refusal to cooperate in the assessment. Thus, while the psychologist and CMO interpreted Peter's behaviour at interview in terms of their clinical diagnosis of a 'personality disorder', the child's account of his behaviour during the interviews was in terms of his expectations of the assessment process itself. The lack of a theoretical framework within which to explore Peter's perspective inhibited these professionals in their evaluation of the information they obtained from their interviews with him. In particular, they were unable to take account of the extent to which this information was influenced by the way Peter interpreted the purpose and possible outcome of the assessment.

Constraints on professionals

The disturbing behaviour of children may arise from tensions in the home or school as well as from personality or constitutional 'disorders'. Nonetheless, psychologists may feel constrained to define the problem in terms of the difficulties the child presents to others despite being sensitive to the influence on the child's behaviour of the context in which it occurs. When a child is referred for assessment this is unlikely to arise solely from a disinterested concern to establish if the child has special educational needs. Reasons for referral will also be related to teachers' expectations of the outcome of the referral. These might include the acquisition of additional resources, the removal of a troublesome child, or a promise to act quickly if matters deteriorate in the future. Thus educational psychologists do not *and cannot* simply assess the child, they must also respond to the teachers' legitimate expectation of receiving a professional service. In practice, therefore, psychologists may feel constrained to negotiate a solution that is acceptable to the school because the school is also their 'client'. In this sense, the LEA, too, is the psychologist's client since its expectation is that the advice of the psychologist will assist in the allocation of scarce resources.

The Department of Education and Science (1989a) asserts that assessments should be carried out without regard to the type of provision available within the LEA. Yet psychologists may encounter pressures that make consideration of the availability of resources difficult to avoid. In one recent case, an educational psychologist insisted on including in his report to parents a brief paragraph explaining that his assessments for the LEA under the 1981 Act required him to advise on their child's needs, not to make recommendations as to how and where those needs should be met. His refusal to comply with an LEA directive to remove this paragraph led to his dismissal, and although an industrial tribunal subsequently found in his favour, he was not reinstated (Pyke, 1990). While there was no reason to suspect that the psychologists in our own study were under such explicit pressure from their LEAs there was evidence that they recognised the need to consider the realities of available provision in making their recommendations if their professional credibility with their school and LEA clients was to be maintained. Acceptance that there were realities which put constraints on the range of recommendations that could effectively be made did not prevent psychologists from actively pushing at the limits of these 'realities'. However, psychologists did frequently find themselves having to balance the various interests of different 'clients'. Each of these clients – child, parents, teachers and LEA – might have legitimate expectations of the psychologist but each might also have potentially conflicting interests. In this situation an assessment of special educational needs could become transformed into conflict resolution. The consequent ethical and professional dilemmas could seriously affect the ability of the psychologist to represent the interests of any or all of these clients (Armstrong and Galloway, 1992b).

The power of the psychologist's different clients to realise their expectations of the assessment will vary. However, where conflict resolution is a major concern of the assessment, the child is likely to be at a disadvantage. This may be so even though the psychologist identifies the child as the principal client. This can be seen, for instance, in the assessment of Matthew, a boy of 15.

Matthew was referred for a formal assessment of his special educational needs following his indefinite exclusion from school on the grounds of aggressive behaviour towards his teachers. The psychologist in this case felt that if Matthew was placed in a special school at such a critical stage in his education he would suffer serious disadvantages because of the limited opportunities that would be available to him for taking GCSEs. Matthew wanted to be readmitted to his school to complete his education, and the psychologist agreed that this was desirable if ground rules could be established with the school:

Because the school excluded Matthew pending psychological assessment I see the preparation of a Statement as a safety net. I do not want to send Matthew to a special school if possible because I believe he can cope with a normal curriculum. I want to say to Matthew's school that a Statement is being prepared so I can recommend that he is readmitted with a behavioural contract.

For their part, the school refused to entertain this proposal. As an alternative, Matthew asked if he could transfer to a different mainstream school in the district. Again the psychologist felt this to be in Matthew's interests. However, after initial enquiries he became aware that Matthew's reputation had travelled before him and other schools in the area were unwilling to accept him. Thus the psychologist finally reported:

I've given up trying to negotiate this. There are only three secondary schools in the area and they do not want to take another school's problem children. For a short time one of the schools was prepared to do this and this was certainly the best of the three. The problem was it got a bad reputation because of the children it took in so it started to suffer from falling rolls. Recently it's got a new head and he's tightened up on admissions.

In these circumstances the psychologist felt he had no real option but to recommend a special school placement for Matthew.

Matthew's case illustrates how the assessment may become focused on the child, either as 'problem' or 'victim', in consequence of the 'need' to take account of the interests of other participants who have greater power to affect the outcome of the assessment procedures. Thus, even where, as in this case, the psychologist is aware of the child's wishes and is willing to take serious account of them in the assessment, he or she may be prevented from doing so by the expectations other clients have of the appropriate outcome.

Conclusions

It is clear that many psychologists and teachers would like to involve children in decision-making and would welcome initiatives leading to this being undertaken systematically within their LEAs and schools. In practice, however, the advice of the DES is generally left at the door of individual professionals. Perhaps not surprisingly our own research revealed that professionals were concerned about the difficulties of turning good intentions into good practice. In part this suggests a need for specialised training to assist professionals to enhance their skills in this area. The work of Gersch (1987, 1990), who has pioneered the use of child self-report procedures in assessments carried out under the 1981 Education Act, points to one way in which training might be appropriate. Other ways are suggested by the work of psychiatrists and psychologists who have been concerned with the question of *how* to listen to children (Ravenette, 1977; Rutter and Graham, 1968; Tammivaara and Enright, 1986). Recent work on records of achievement and pupil profiling is also of relevance here (Broadfoot, 1986). What is clear from the experience of those who have successfully implemented records of achievement is that the positive cooperation and involvement of teachers, pupils and parents, together with the effectiveness of the schemes in terms of learning outcomes, has depended upon the existence of coherent programmes of in-service training (Garforth, 1986). The importance, demonstrated by this experience, of combining coherent policy with well-informed practice is particularly relevant to attempts to maximise the contribution of children themselves to the assessment of special needs.

However, the genuine concerns that many professionals have about how to encourage the participation of children as partners in the assessment and decision-making processes may tie in with a deeper concern among those professionals, namely that their work in respect of formal assessments under the 1981 Act is frequently reactive. In these circumstances the opportunity to take account of the perspectives of children may be undermined by the 'crisis' that has initiated the assessment. Where this occurs it may not be 'poor practice' that leads to the child's perspective being disregarded, but rather the demands of a complex situation in which the needs of competing clients (school, parents, LEA and child) may determine the extent to which the child's perspective *is allowed to be relevant*. In the absence of a clear policy on the role of the child in the assessment, and of procedures to empower the child, the conflicts of interest that permeate an assessment will continue to inhibit the development of frameworks for partnership with children.

CHAPTER 5

Parents' participation

Introduction

This chapter reviews changes made by the 1981 Education Act to the rights of parents in decision-making about children's special educational needs. The significance of these changes is examined in the light of strong evidence of continuing parental disenchantment with the implementation of this legislation. In looking critically at the philosophy of 'parents as partners' promoted by the Warnock Report (DES, 1978) and central to the 1981 Act, we question the extent to which this philosophy is designed to empower parents. Circumstances are identified where the philosophy of partnership may actually disempower those parents who are most vulnerable. We argue that the ambiguity of professional roles, together with the inadequacy of existing procedures for ensuring that parents' views are properly represented, places parents at a serious disadvantage in their dealings with professionals. By drawing on case study evidence from our research into the assessment of children identified as having emotional and behavioural difficulties, we examine strategies used by parents and professionals to 'negotiate' their own preferred outcomes.

Parents and special education: 1944–1978

The 1944 Education Act introduced procedures under which local authorities were required to provide for the education of handicapped pupils. The Handicapped Pupils and School Health Regulations (MoE, 1945, 1959) made under the 1944 Act identified 11 (later reduced to 10) categories of handicap. This emphasis upon categories of handicap meant that the procedures took the child's 'handicap' as the major criterion to be used for defining educational needs. The subordination of educational needs to medical decision-making had significant implications for the role of parents in the assessment procedures. These procedures focused upon a field of knowledge beyond the expertise of most parents. As such, little or no value might be placed on parents' knowledge of their child in a wide variety of situations. In addition, the dominant part played by medical criteria in the assessment process meant that parents often lacked the knowledge and vocabulary for arguing their views with professionals.

Throughout this period evidence mounted of parents' dissatisfaction with the role they were given in the assessment process. Tomlinson's study of the assessment of 40 children identified as 'educationally subnormal' (Tomlinson, 1981a) highlighted the sense of confusion and isolation felt by many parents who reported being given insufficient information about how and why decisions had been taken. Tomlinson argued that, to a large extent, this situation arose because different professions used different criteria in making their recommendations, and that these were more closely related to perceptions of their own professional roles and interests than informed by any 'objective' or consistent criteria. The conflict between professional groups who increasingly came into competition for control over the assessment procedures significantly contributed, she maintained, to the particular form of label attached to disadvantaged groups and individuals.

Dyson drew similar conclusions from her research carried out in 1982, one year before the 1981 Education Act was implemented, on the assessment of 20 children identified as severely educationally subnormal. Dyson (1986, p. 75) argued that the assessment procedures were frequently a

charade which the professionals play, seeking to persuade both themselves and others that they actually have something to offer the clients.

The secrecy of the assessment process was something she identified as particularly disturbing. Since information can be transferred freely between professionals without parents being given access to it, the power of professionals is enhanced and hence their own role as decision-makers legitimised without necessarily contributing anything to the child's benefit.

By the end of the 1970s parents were becoming increasingly vocal about their frustrations with the special education system (Booth and Statham, 1982). A study by Hannam (1975), who was himself the parent of a mentally handicapped child, drew attention to how the exclusion of parents by professionals at an early stage in the decision-making process can have long-term effects on their willingness and ability to participate in future decisions about their children, and can

leave the individual family unit with a feeling of helplessness and despair.

(Hannam, 1975, p. 116)

Warnock and after

The Warnock Report (DES, 1978) was seen by many as enshrining the principle of parent–professional partnership in special education. Indeed, a whole chapter of the report was dedicated to this topic alone. One of its main recommendations was that professionals should carry out their assessment of a child's needs in partnership with the child's parents. Thus, to facilitate such a partnership it was argued that parents should have a right of access to *all* information collected during the course of an assessment.

Reflecting on the significance of the report when the 1981 Education Act had taken effect, Mary Warnock laid particular emphasis on the effects of the chapter on parents as partners:

The involvement of parents in the whole process of decision-making with regard to the education of their children will, I believe, inevitably tend to improve provision. . . . But, more importantly, teachers and officers will now have to be able to demonstrate that there is no child allowed simply to sit in school with education going on all around him, from which he cannot benefit. No child is ineducable; and parents now have a right to demand that their child shall be genuinely and properly educated. (Warnock, 1982, p.xx)

The precise nature of professional accountability to parents is less clearly spelt out. Despite its rhetoric there is little evidence in the report that parents are seen as having any independent decision-making role. Great emphasis is placed on parents' need for support and advice from professionals yet the rationale for providing such support is not that of creating conditions in which parents can make informed decisions. Rather, it is argued that parental cooperation is essential if the effectiveness of professional interventions are to be maximised. Parents are acknowledged as likely to be the principal carers with day-to-day responsibility for meeting the child's needs. Thus, parents' partnership with professionals is seen as essential if they are to be adequately equipped for putting the advice of professionals into effect. This reflects a social welfare model of provision for special educational needs based on professional expertise and benevolence.

Perhaps recognising the confusion that arose from the concept of parents as partners in the report, Warnock (1985) tried to clarify the point:

In our 1978 report on the Education of Children with Special Needs we had a chapter entitled 'Parents as Partners', in which we urged teachers to take seriously the parental understanding of the handicapped child, and to treat parents as equals. I think, looking back, we exaggerated. For in educational matters, parents cannot be the equals to teachers if teachers are to be regarded as true professionals. Even though educating a child is a joint enterprise, involving both home and school, parents should realise that they cannot have the last word. It is a question of collaboration not partnership.

(Warnock, 1985, p.12)

The 1981 Education Act

The 1981 Education Act is in fact far less explicit about the notion of partnership between professionals and parents than is often assumed.

The Act, nonetheless, did establish a number of new parental rights in law. These rights are principally concerned with access to information, although Section 9(1) for the first time gives parents the right to request that an assessment be carried out, and this is a request that must be complied with unless the LEA considers that it would be unreasonable to do so.

Where an assessment is to be undertaken, Section 5(3) of the Act imposes a duty on the LEA to inform parents fully of the procedures to be followed in the assessment. Parents must also be informed of their right to make representations to the LEA within a 29-day minimum period following the date of being notified that the assessment is to take place. Para. 2(4) of Schedule 1 to the Act gives parents the right to be present during their child's examination by psychologist and doctor. Section 7(3) requires the LEA to submit a draft Statement to parents specifying the proposals they wish to make for meeting a child's special educational needs if such needs have been identified. This draft Statement must be accompanied by copies of the professional, parental and other advice which the LEA has used in formulating its recommendations. Under this section of the Act parents must also be informed of their right to make representations to the LEA on the advice. If, after discussions with an officer of the LEA, differences have not been resolved to parents' satisfaction, they may appeal to a local appeals tribunal. This tribunal may recommend that the LEA reconsiders its decision but it does not have the power to overrule the LEA. However, parents do now have a new right of appeal to the Secretary of State for Education.

It is to the advice of the Department of Education and Science (1983, 1989a) on the implementation of the Act that we must turn to find elaboration of the principle of partnership between parents and professionals. Here it is maintained that

The relations between professional advisers and parents during the process of assessment are of crucial importance. Parents should be encouraged to feel that they are partners in the process. (DES, 1989a, para. 49)

The status of DES circulars is purely advisory and therefore the practice of parent–professional partnership may vary widely from authority to authority. As we argue in the next section, the translation of statutory parental rights into a policy involving a genuine partnership between professionals and parents is no straightforward matter. This is evident from parents' negative experiences of the assessment process that continue to emerge quite consistently from across the whole country (see Goacher *et al.*, 1988).

In two studies of parents' views abour special education placements, Swann (1984), one year after the implementation of the 1981 Act, found evidence that where the parents' beliefs about placement conflicted with those of the LEA and its advisers it was generally parents' experience that they 'must accept partnership on their opposite partner's terms' (p. 10). Sharron (1985) reviewed a number of cases which, he argued, suggest that the flow of information to parents may be manipulated in ways that undermine their power to make informed decisions. Research recently carried out into the implementation of similar legislation in Scotland (Riddell *et al.*, 1990) found evidence of professionals retaining control over the assessment procedures by failing to provide parents with adequate information, excluding them from multi-professional meetings and omitting to foster the involvement of voluntary organisations and named persons. A lack of information about the assessment is likely to limit the effectiveness of all parents who may be involved in these procedures, but there is evidence that some parents suffer more disadvantage in this respect than others. Chaudhury (1986) and Rehal (1989) have both observed that language and cultural differences, on occasions together with overt racism, may leave parents from ethnic minority communities confused and powerless. Rehal (1989), for instance, has shown how children may be placed in special schools while their parents are unaware that an assessment of special educational needs has taken place, let alone having been given the opportunity to contribute to it.

Goacher *et al.* (1988), in a national review of the implementation of the 1981 Act, found evidence of widespread parental dissatisfaction with the quality of information they received and the level of involvement they were allowed in the decision-making process. The difficulties parents encountered in these respects were compounded by the great diversity of ways in which different LEAs chose to interpret and implement the Act. Moreover, the absence in many LEAs of any clear statement of policy in this area meant that parents were uncertain what to expect from an assessment and were heavily reliant on the individual professionals with whom they had direct contact. In this idiosyncratic and confusing theatre of local authority policy, the chances of finding consistent criteria being used to identify children with special educational needs – and against which parents can evaluate the effectiveness of professional intervention and local authority provision – are slim. Indeed, some researchers have argued that the 1981 Act may be used to secure outcomes that have little to do with a child's educational needs, but which do provide an administratively easier way of dealing with 'social problems'. Malek (1990), for instance, found strong evidence in two LEAs of residential school placements being used as an alternative to the placement of children in residential care. The former were seen by these LEAs as more acceptable to parents although the standards of evidence required for such placements are far less rigorous than those applied by the juvenile court.

Barriers to partnership

The picture painted thus far is gloomy, suggesting that the spirit of the 1981 Act is consistently being thwarted by the actions of LEAs and their professional advisers, with the latter using the assessment procedures to maintain their own professional authority and power. In nearly all the cases investigated in our own research there was some evidence to support this, particularly from the parent's perspective. There was considerable evidence of parents' dissatisfaction with their treatment by professionals and LEAs. These parents also perceived themselves to have little control over the assessment procedures and decisions taken regarding their outcome. Indeed, of the 29 cases studied, in only five did parents express themselves as being content with the outcome and satisfied with their involvment in making decisions about their children's futures. However, parents, including those who were satisfied with the outcome of the assessment, invariably complained that they had been denied access to full and up-to-date information when they needed it to make informed decisons. To some extent this reflected poor communication rather than an intent to mislead, although our own independent observations leant support to claims of misinformation in at least two of the cases we studied. Clearly in some cases issues were raised about the quality of professional practice. While it would be fairly easy for us to identify and criticise instances of poor practice, we believe it is more interesting, and ultimately more important, to examine those factors that limit and inhibit the participation of parents in the assessment procedures even where professionals are committed to facilitating genuine parent–professional cooperation and partnership. Our research method gave us a unique opportunity to observe the many different parts of each child's assessment as well as interviewing all the key participants about their perceptions at each stage. This allowed us insight into the complex social interactions between parents and professionals that gave rise to the former's experiences. In particular, by following children through all the main stages of their assessment we were able to see beyond the common and naive stereotypes of professionals that appear in much of the literature on this subject.

In the remainder of this chapter we identify three themes emerging from our research. The first illustrates how ambiguities in professional roles may lead to the disempowerment of parents *even where professionals are committed to involving parents in decision-making*. The second theme examines how power embedded in professional roles may lead to outcomes being imposed and/or negotiated which reinforce the subordinate role of parents. The third theme looks at strategies used by parents to obtain genuine power in their negotiations with professionals.

Ambiguities in professional roles

The role of the psycholgist in assessments under the 1981 Education Act is ambiguous. This ambiguity arises because different people involved in the assessment have a legitimate expectation that the psychologist will provide them with a service. In consequence, conflict and/or confusion may be difficult to avoid. This conflict places constraints on the role that parents are *allowed* to have in the decison-making process. How this may occur is illustrated in Ben's assessment.

Ben was one of the children participating in our research on the assessment process. He was technically on the role of a mainstream primary school but had been placed full time in an off-site unit for children with behavioural difficulties since the age of seven. Although he had been seen by a psychologist at the time of his admission to the unit, a Statement of special educational needs had never been made, nor had a full assessment been carried out. Now, at the age of 10, his teachers in the unit, in consultation with an educational psychologist, felt that an attempt should be made to reintegrate him into a mainstream school. The agreement of Ben's parents to this proposal was obtained, a host school identified and a trial period of reintegration started, initially for one day each week. Ben seemed to settle well into his new school and following further discussions with his parents a full-time placement at the school was proposed. However, teachers at the host school were anxious about the possible implications of accepting Ben full time and refused to do so unless they were provided with a full-time classroom assistant to supervise him. They believed it was important that their willingness to take on board a 'difficult' pupil should be acknowledged by the LEA in the form of additional resources.

This was a request the LEA was reluctant to grant without a Statement of special educational needs having been made for fear of setting a precedent. The psychologist had been told that:

If a short-term assistant is put in it may be very difficult to withdraw as parents may manipulate a temporary arrangement.

The Statementing procedures were seen by the LEA, therefore, as providing a system of administrative checks on the distribution of resources.

The psychologist in this case was sensitive to the different needs of the child, parents, school and LEA, yet he believed a formula for Ben's reintegration into mainstream could be achieved that would be acceptable to all of them. This, he argued, would require Ben's special educational needs to be formally assessed under the provisions of the 1981 Act and, on the assumption that this would lead to a successful reintegration being achieved, Ben's parents agreed to go along with the proposal. Later, they became concerned that their agreement might have left them powerless to resist the LEA if at the end of the assessment it was decided that Ben should be placed in a special school rather than in a mainstream school. His mother reflected on this possibility, when we interviewed her.

I thought the reason for a statement was to force the authority's hand. . . . That's why I agreed to start the statementing. Afterwards I thought it through myself and was concerned about the possibility of it backfiring.

As the procedures rumbled on over a period of 9 months Ben's parents felt that they had little control over events and, in consequence, became distrustful of the psychologist's motives. Their anxieties were not lessened by the refusal of the psychologist to provide any guarantees about the outcome of the assessment even though, in this authority, he had the administrative responsibility for drafting the proposed Statement. He believed that to do so would have been to compromise his professional integrity in the eyes of the LEA, who employed him and looked to him for independent professional advice. From the LEA's perspective the role of the psychologist was to provide them with advice that would assist their decision-making about the efficient management of resources.

The ambiguities inherent in the psychologist's professional role meant that he had to be responsive to the expectations of all his clients. Yet because these clients had potentially conflicting interests both his advocacy and his consultancy roles became problematic. Conscious of how the conflicting expectations placed constraints on the advice he was able to offer, his main concern became that of reconciling the interests of these 'clients' rather than simply carrying out a clinical assessment of Ben's needs and making recommendations based on 'objective' evidence about how these needs could best be met.

Initially Ben's parents had seen the psychologist as their advocate, offering advice on how to achieve their shared objectives. As the assessment unfolded they became more aware of the psychologist's role as an officer of the LEA and the constraints this placed on his advocacy role. In particular, they were suspicious that negotiations were taking place and decisions made over matters about which they were being given no say. Yet, by now, they felt dependent upon the psychologist and powerless to take any independent action for fear of damaging the chances of a successful outcome being reached. This sense of disempowerment is strongly expressed in a discussion Ben's mother, Mrs Lee, had with the psychologist some 9 months after the Statementing procedures began:

Mrs Lee: The possibility of Ben going to school in September may not happen now because of the delay.
Psych.: He may not go in September but he may not have gone anyway.

Mrs Lee: Maybe I misunderstood it but if the Statement says he needs it, he has a legal right to receive it.

Psych.: Once its signed by the education officer, but he may decide not to sign it.

Mrs Lee: On what grounds?

Psych.: If he did not have a classroom assistant available.

Mrs Lee: So its down to politics and money really. . . . I've got to the stage where I see time running out for Ben. I'm getting to the stage of simply removing him from the unit. I might not get him into a school but I'll have to go round knocking on doors. I might have to keep him at home and then the Education will have to do something about it.

Psych.: If you do that it might undermine the case we have been pushing for so long.

Mrs Lee: You've got to understand, I did leave it in the psychological service's hand but they filed it and forgot about it. That doesn't give you much confidence. Once this Statementing was first mentioned to me it was a very big thing and it frightened me but now the system's failed.

Psych.: I don't want you to do something that will make things more likely to fail.

Mrs Lee: If I pulled Ben out of the unit would the Statement cease to exist?

Psych.: The Statementing process would continue. If the education officer is told that you have taken Ben out of the unit I don't know how he will react. He might say 'the child's out of school and out of school he's violent. It might be harder for him to fit back into mainstream.' It would certainly jeopardise *our* case.

Commenting on this meeting shortly after it was over the psychologist expressed considerable sympathy for Mrs Lee and irritation that it had been necessary to go through the Statementing procedures at all in order to obtain classroom support for Ben. It was, he said,

a matter of satisfying the school's needs, not the child's. A lower level of support would have been adequate for Ben but I felt I couldn't be seen to be negotiating it down by the school.

Yet his sympathies for the difficult position in which Mrs Lee now found herself were tempered by his awareness that his own credibility as an adviser to the school and the LEA depended upon his willingness to negotiate outcomes that did not compromise their interests.

Bewildered by what was happening and by her loss of control over events, Mrs Lee was deeply concerned about what the outcome of the assessment would be. In her view Ben's interests were being damaged, but she believed she was now powerless to do anything about it:

If I had the courage I would take him out of the unit and try to get him into another mainstream school myself, but I feel my hands are tied – they've left me with no options.

Partnership and power

A consistent theme in our interviews with parents was the inequality, as they perceived it, in their relationship with professionals. At face value the assessment procedures are governed by a set of legal rules which recognise the expertise of parents and guarantee their right to participate in decision-making about their children's needs in partnership with professionals. These are the rules that parents are made aware of at the outset of an assessment under the 1981 Act, and they are the parents' guide to procedures as they unfold. It is in terms of these rules that parents are expected (and allowed) to make sense of the assessment process. Yet, the rules comprise only a part of parents' experience of the social processes inherent in an assessment.

In addition to the formal rules there is also an assessment 'culture'. This is a professional culture to which parents have only limited access. The 'assessment culture', like all cultures, is built up over time through the interactions taking place within a community. It is this culture that provides the meanings within which the formal rules are understood and applied. It is a professional culture, if only because professionals are consistently involved in its development and elaboration. Parents come and go. They are involved in the negotiation of meanings within the culture, but with each new assessment new parents become the participants, and their ignorance of the cultural context within which the negotiations takes place puts parents continually at a disadvantage. They lack the cultural memory that might give them access to power. Professionals, on the other hand, by virtue of their continuing participation in the assessment process from one case to another, build up shared understandings of this process with their fellow professionals which guide their actions and interactions. This cultural memory enables professionals to convey and make sense of hidden agendas lying behind the formal procedures.

The inequality between professionals and parents, embedded in the culture of assessment, may be contrasted with situations involving interprofessional negotiations. Professionals such as psychologists and teachers are more accountable to their professional colleagues for their actions and decisions precisely because those colleagues are party to the cultural norms that predicate the negotiations. Thus, psychologists' professional clients are better able to negotiate outcomes which they find satisfactory than are their non-professional clients (Armstrong and Galloway, 1992b).

Where parents attempt to use the official procedures of the assessment to achieve the outcomes they desire, their ignorance of the culture of the assessment – a culture implicit in the practice of professionals but not necessarily articulated – may result in their participation becoming a source of their disempowerment. At the same time other, professional, participants may use their cultural knowledge to empower themselves in negotiations both with parents and with other professionals. The empowerment and disempowerment of professional and parent participants through the assessment culture can be seen in two further cases from our research.

Following allegations made to Ian's teachers by his natural father, the Peel family were visited by a community nurse. After a visit to the family home this nurse wrote a report in which she concluded that there was evidence of sexual abuse within the family. The 'evidence' was decidedly limited and was based almost entirely on the child's behaviour. The primary school which the Peel children attended was also concerned about the behaviour of Ian and his sister and when they received a copy of the community nurse's report, Ian, but not his sister, was referred to the schools' psychological service for an assessment of his special educational needs. Although the evidence of abuse was thin, and a later investigation by the social services department revealed no justification for intervention, the educational psychologist felt that these issues were beyond his area of professional concern and that 'we have to accept what we are told about his behaviour by his teachers'. This view, not surprisingly, had significant consequences for the subsequent role of both parents and professionals in the assessment process.

From the perspectives of professionals and of parents, there was a breakdown in any idea of partnership in meeting the child's needs. According to the professionals the breakdown occurred because the parents were the cause of their children's problems. Consequently, they defined cooperation in terms that would enable them

to intervene within the family and explore the deficits in the parenting role.

The Peels were expected to accept the professionals' authority even though there was little evidence to support the allegations. Yet, had the parents cooperated with the professionals this would have implied their acceptance of the professionals' views that they were inadequate parents. On the other hand, their refusal to cooperate would also have been interpreted as evidence of their inadequacy as parents. This was a case in which parents could not win and shows how assumptions about parental deficits may become implicit in the culture of the assessment process to the extent that parent–professional 'partnership' operates to deny parents a genuine role in decision-making.

A second example of how the culture of assessment may operate to disempower parents occurred after George was referred to the schools' psychological service by his teachers because of his behaviour at school. They were pressing to have George transferred to a special school and on the referral form concern was expressed about his home situation. In this case the most crucial negotiations were those that took place between the psychologist and George's teachers, leading to his referral for assessment being accepted by the LEA. These negotiations focused upon the reports given by George's teachers about his home situation. On the basis of these the psychologist formed the opinion that George's needs could not be met either in a mainstream school or in a day special school (though at no time prior to this decision or during the assessment did the psychologist visit the home to observe George's behaviour or talk to his parents).

George's parents were unaware of this background when they were asked whether they had any objections to the assessment taking place. Their agreement to the assessment was based upon their own concerns about a deteriorating school situation in which they believed George was being treated unfairly by his teachers. Once the assessment began, it was quite clear that its main focus would be on the family and Mr and Mrs Short's parenting skills. The assumption was that difficulties at home were causing problems for George's teachers with his behaviour in school. No assessment was made by the psychologist or anyone else of how George's learning and behaviour had been managed in school by his teachers.

These parents did accept that George could be difficult to handle at home and said that they would like help and advice, but they were insistent that the main problem was the attitude of his teachers towards the family and that nothing was to be gained by sending George to a residential school. They were particularly concerned about this latter possibility because of what they claimed had been the damaging effects on relationships within their family following the decision to send George's elder brother, Stuart, to a residential school for children with moderate learning difficulties. Prior to this placement, they maintained that Stuart's *behaviour* at home was good. Now 'when he comes home he's a lot worse'. This change in their son's behaviour was interpreted by them as signalling his sense of rejection by the family. George's psychologist was unimpressed by this argument, believing it was more likely that Stuart's changed behaviour at home reflected a deteriorating family environment and therefore added weight to his recommendation that George also should be sent to a residential school.

This psychologist did, however, express a strong belief that it was important to help parents make decisions. Helping parents to arrive at decisions 'they really want to make' was acknowledged as a task involving complex skills and great sensitivity. Thus, when George's parents suggested that both they and George needed some time apart for a holiday this was interpreted as meaning that they couldn't cope with George at home but did not want to appear responsible for sending him away to school because of the guilt they felt having done this already with Stuart.

On the basis of this interpretation the psychologist, in recommending in his report a residential school placement for George, stated that this recommendation was supported by George's parents. The psychologist had not discussed his interpretation of what they were saying with them, yet their acquiescence with the recommendation when it was included in the proposed Statement of special educational needs was taken as demonstrating its validity.

George's parents made no formal objection to the LEA's decision. Nonetheless, they were adamant throughout the assessment that this outcome was not what they wanted. Indeed, they insisted that 'it's going to make him worse'. They did acknowledge, both in discussions with the psychologist and in interviews with us, that they needed support as a family. Only at the end of the assessment, when they knew that the type of support they wanted would not be given, did they become resigned to the inevitability of decisions being taken by the professionals irrespective of their own wishes:

We've come to our own conclusions about what is going on. They want him out.

We would suggest that the most interesting feature of this case is not that the wishes of the professionals prevailed over those of parents; rather it shows how the subordinate role of parents may be imposed through attempts to give parents a voice in decisions. In acting to facilitate the decision-making power of parents, the psychologist appeared unaware of the extent to which power, embedded in his own role by the assessment culture, inhibited his ability to explore points of difference between his own beliefs about the parents' wishes and what they were actually saying. How different participants perceive their own role and the roles of others, together with the status, power and rights seen to derive from those roles, are important factors establishing the expectations of any interaction between them. Who makes the referral for assessment? Who is seen to have knowledge and expertise? What sorts of knowledge and expertise are valued and why? Who controls the distribution of information? Differences between the perspectives of parents and professionals cannot be seen in isolation from actual and perceived relationships of power. Thus, it is rarely enough for professionals to have a moral commitment to working in partnership with parents.

The fact that so few parents turn discontent into opposition perhaps suggests that, for their part, parents are more conscious of the inequality embedded in the culture of the assessment than are their professional partners. Invariably at the outset of their children's assessments the parents in our study believed they would have *the* major role in decision-making. Yet, where parents tried to exercise this decision-making power within the assessment procedures their attempts were frustrated by the lack of alternatives with which they were presented. By contrast, there were parents who, by actions they took outside the assessment process, found ways of empowering themselves so that their negotiations with professionals took place on a more equal footing. It is to these parents that we now turn.

Stepping outside the Act

As we have seen, the 1981 Education Act gives many new rights to parents, yet parents may still feel unable to exercise their rights in any meaningful way. On the other hand, this does not imply that professionals deliberately manipulate parents into accepting decisions with which those parents are unhappy. Conspiracy theories of this sort reflect a naive oversimplification of what in reality are very complex processes of social interaction. Moreover, despite the picture sometimes painted in the literature, our own research suggests that parents rarely accept a subordinate role without a fight and invoke various strategies in an attempt to empower themselves in the assessment process.

Thus, in at least seven of the 29 cases we followed, parents tried to influence the outcome by obtaining and using information from sources other than their professional advisers. In five cases parents promoted and/or exploited dissent between professionals to strengthen their own bargaining position in the assessment. In three cases parents attempted to remove their children from schools with whom they were in dispute. As we shall see, this strategy could be particularly effective, but it was also one that was strongly resisted by professionals.

The relative success of strategies used by parents was quite variable. For instance, some parents were able to achieve limited gains such as speeding-up the assessment process. Nonetheless, whatever the strength of parental objections to professional recommendations it remains the case that where these were pursued through the official channels of the 1981 Act procedures they were in each case unsuccessful. By contrast, in five cases parents made very determined efforts to challenge the authority of the professionals and LEA by taking matters into their own hands. None of these cases went to appeal but in three cases parents successfully forced the outcome they wanted against the advice and recommendations of the professionals. In the other two cases parents did not achieve their initial objectives but a compromise was reached which they felt to be a significant improvement on the LEA's initial proposals.

One mother obtained a place for her son in a residential school in spite of the LEA's initial reluctance to agree to this. She was able to obtain agreement by using information provided by a friend who worked at the school, and by persuading her MP to make a complaint to the LEA. She reported that

The psychologist saw Stephen a few times at school and thought that an assessment should be started because he had special educational needs, but when he was expelled they couldn't care less as long as he was out of school.

Six months later Stephen was still out of school and the assessment had not started but

within 24 hours of getting a letter from the MP the authority had started the assessment. They're still not concerned about Stephen, they're concerned that the MP is going to make this public. One minute they didn't want to do anything, next they couldn't spend enough money.

Another parent expressed little confidence in her 'rights' under the Act when an educational psychologist recommended a residential school placement. She moved house, and with the cooperation of the head teacher of a school near to her new home, withdrew her son from the off-site unit for disruptive pupils which he had previously been attending part time, so that he could attend the new mainstream school full time. According to Mrs Jones, the LEA had little option in the circumstances but to allow her decision 'the chance to fail'. It seems a pity that she could only obtain this chance by moving house. As we shall see, however, this was not the only case where parents chose to move house in order to make the LEA listen to their views about their child's needs. In taking action outside the official assessment procedures to obtain an outcome which they considered acceptable, these parents were highly sceptical of the role of their professional advisers. They were very conscious of the pressure the latter were under to deliver outcomes that would be acceptable to their professional 'partners', including teachers and LEA administrators. In this respect, they clearly understood that there was a difference between the rhetoric of partnership contained in the Act and the reality of negotiation for resources. Sometimes this was a lesson learnt during the assessment itself.

Susan was referred to the schools' psychological service by her primary school after her teachers became concerned about her behaviour in school following an indecent assault by an elderly neighbour. They described her as 'attention seeking' and were particularly worried by her deliberate attempts to induce vomiting so that she would be sent home from school. The class teacher considered that the assault had had a serious emotional effect on Susan and was perplexed because no one, in her view, seemed to be taking it seriously.

Susan's parents were concerned about her behaviour in school but suggested that this was more likely caused by the emotional overreaction of her teacher than by the assault. They pointed out that her behaviour at home was not difficult and they were concerned that, in their opinion, Susan was being blamed for the failings of her teacher.

When Susan was seen by an educational psychologist he felt sympathy with her parents' criticisms of the class teacher but was reluctant to adopt an advocacy role on their behalf:

I agree that the parents did feel the problem to be school- specific. From what they were saying things in Susan's previous school were just fine – no problems at all. Certainly Susan's difficulties may have increased because of school-specific reasons. I do know the school and I do know that teacher, and really I agree with the parents about the teacher, though of course it would have been quite unprofessional of me to tell them that.

The psychologist carried out a psychometric assessment and found evidence that Susan had some mild learning difficulties. He concluded in his report that these were likely to be the reason for Susan's difficulties in school, making no mention of his views about possible 'school-specific' reasons for Susan's difficulties. Susan's parents accepted that she was behind in her school work but believed this had more to do with poor teaching than with any intellectual impairment. The psychologist, however, in forming his own assessment of Susan's needs attempted to distance himself from the conflict between parents and school while working with the school to renegotiate their perceptions of Susan's difficulties and the reasons for them. Although this strategy may have been the most effective way of addressing the needs of Susan's teachers, her parents felt that their own concerns were not being treated seriously by any of the professionals involved in the assessment.

We believe Susan is just a sensitive child. If you show her kindness she'll do anything for you, but who's going to believe me? I'm just a mother.

Time went on, and receiving no feedback on the progress of the assessment they became increasingly anxious about the likely outcome of the assessment. Nothing appeared to have been done about the situation they believed was causing Susan such unhappiness in school, and Susan's parents felt unable to influence the progress and outcome of the assessment:

We sat back and let it take its course.

Yet this perception of the role they were given in the assessment contrasted sharply with the action they took in an effort to resolve the difficulties Susan was encountering in school. They made a decision to move house and transfer Susan to a new primary school. They were advised against this by the psychologist who felt that the assessment would lead to Susan's receiving extra help to compensate for her intellectual disabilities. It was argued by the psychologist that if her education was disrupted now by a change of school the effectiveness of this help would be reduced. Susan's parents, believing that the assessment would have little bearing on the 'real problem', rejected this advice.

Once the change of school had been made, Susan's parents noted almost immediate improvements in her behaviour at school and in the quality of her school work. According to her father, one term after the move, her problem behaviour

seems pretty remote. It were all the other school.

This was a view that seems to have been shared by Susan's new teacher who observed that Susan had easily made friends in school although this had come

as some surprise. When I read the reports it said she'd had difficulty in making friends. I think she coped admirably with the situation.

Conclusions

Despite the official endorsement of a 'parents as partners' philosophy in the 1981 Education Act, in practice parents continue to complain that they are denied the power that would make their contribution to the decision-making process meaningful and equal. As Kirp (1983) has argued, the denial of real power to parents stems as much from the ideology of benevolent professionalism that has dominated thinking about children with special needs in this country as it does from any lack of legal rights.

In this chapter we have looked at some of the consequences of this ideology and, in particular, at how partnership with professionals may itself lead to a loss of power for parents. For their part, professionals may be unaware of the extent to which the cultural context of the assessment operates to disempower parents. Moreover, genuine partnership between parents and professionals may be impossible while demands are placed on professionals by different clients with different and potentially conflicting expectations of professional roles. Recognising the inequality of their position within the assessment, parents may seek ways of securing for themselves a more powerful role in decision-making by locating that process within a cultural context with which they are more familiar. The extent to which parents are successful in achieving outcomes that they find acceptable may ultimately rest upon their willingness to challenge directly the power of professionals by action outside the formal procedures of the assessment.

CHAPTER 6

Educational psychologists: educationalists, clinicians or resource gatekeepers?

Introduction

The 1944 Education Act triggered 30 years of increasing friction between educational psychologists and school medical officers. At the heart of the problem lay formal 'ascertainment' that a child was 'suffering' from one of the statutory categories of handicap. The Act placed responsibility for ascertainment on doctors for two reasons: first, handicaps, including serious learning and behavioural difficulties, were still seen as a medical rather than as an educational problem; second, the fledgling profession of educational psychology contained insufficient members to cope with the growing volume of work.

The 30 years following the 1944 Act saw dramatic increases in the numbers of children placed in special schools. In most LEA's all these children underwent formal ascertainment, in spite of the facts that this was not required by the Act, and that successive Ministry of Education and DES circulars had indicated that it was unnecessary except when the LEA wished to enforce attendance at a special school against parental wishes (Galloway and Goodwin, 1979, 1987). Many doctors recognised formal ascertainment as a symbol of their authority and resented the attempts of educational psychologists in the expanding school psychological services to invade their territory. LEA officers, meanwhile, stood on the sidelines, watching the two professions bicker and squabble over individual cases. By 1975 sufficient consensus had emerged on the importance of educational advice in reaching decisions over special educational provision. A further and more explicit DES circular (1975) recommended multidisciplinary assessment, with a clear implication that LEAs should be seeking advice on educational placement from educational psychologists.

The 1981 Education Act made multidisciplinary assessment a statutory requirement whenever a LEA wished to issue a Statement of a child's special educational needs. Advice from an educational psychologist formed part of this multidisciplinary assessment, but responsibility for decisions about what resources should be provided, and where they should be provided, was placed firmly with the LEAs. Subsequent circulars (DES, 1983, 1989a) made clear that educational psychologists should identify children's needs, but should not concern themselves with how, or even whether, they could be met. Therein lay a dilemma which still proves virtually impossible to resolve, and continues to exert a malign effect on the professional practice of educational psychologists.

In theory, educational psychologists are merely one part of a multidisciplinary team. In practice, their training appears to give them a pre-eminent place within this team. It includes an Honours Degree in psychology, a teaching qualification, at least two years' teaching and a post-graduate degree or diploma in applied educational psychology. Unlike any other member of the multidisciplinary team, the educational psychologist has specific professional training in the assessment of special educational needs. Unsurprisingly, then, LEAs did not only look to their psychologists for advice on the nature of children's special educational needs; they also look to them for advice on how these needs should be met.

For two reasons, the DES advice (1983, 1989a) that psychologists should identify needs rather than advise on how and where they should be met was never credible. First, it ignored the logic of the 1981 Act itself. Second, it also treated with lofty indifference the pressures facing LEAs as they struggled to accommodate a decade of educational reform. We shall take these points separately,

1. In theory, the 1981 Act recognised that special educational needs was a relative concept, not an absolute one. Whether a child had learning difficulties requiring extra support or alternative provision depended on other factors. On *theoretical and logical* grounds, we cannot assess children's special educational needs without having regard to factors which may affect their progress and behaviour. In other words, one has to assess special needs in the context in which they become apparent.

    How far the 'context' extends is not straightforward. Obviously, it includes the resources available to a teacher. More controversially, it also includes the use he or she makes of them. This implies the need for an evaluative judgement of the quality of teaching a child is receiving. Less obviously, the context in which assessment takes place must also include the teacher's and the head teacher's beliefs about how children's needs should be met. These beliefs, in turn, will be influenced by the pressures under which they feel themselves to be working, and by their knowledge of special provision which the authority can make available, either within or outside the mainstream. The DES' (1983,1989a) tidy administrative solution that pychologists should distinguish between identification of a child's needs and decisions about how and where they should be met could never stand up to scrutiny.

2. It also overlooked the pressures on LEAs. Children have a legal right to the educational resources specified in a Statement. LEAs have to provide these resources from a finite sum of money. They

cannot simply phone the Secretary of State or increase the council tax if it runs out. Indeed, if the council does increase the council tax it could find itself 'capped', and thus forced by central government to reduce spending incurred by Acts of Parliament passed by this same government. In relation to the 1981 Act, LEAs found themselves trapped in a pincer movement. One arm consisted of increasingly articulate, well-informed and determined parents. The other consisted of similarly articulate, well-informed and determined head teachers. In this impossible situation, to whom could hard-pressed LEA officers turn for advice about the distribution of finite resources? Obviously, educational psychologists!

The remainder of this chapter will draw on our own research to illustrate the pressures on educational psychologists, and show how they respond to these pressures. We shall give a brief description of psychologists' involvement with children whose assessments we followed. We shall then draw on case histories to throw light on the nature of the role conflict they experience and to identify the different models of professional relationships with which they necessarily operate, but which often result in confusion for parents and other clients. This will show that the process leading to psychologists' decisions – or, more properly, recommendations – is infinitely more complex than is often believed.

Assessment by educational psychologists

We are concerned here only with the part that educational psychologists play in the formal assessment of special educational needs as required by the 1981 Education Act. We shall argue, though, that the advice they provide is necessarily influenced by factors unconnected with the child in question. Educational psychologists cannot carry out assessments of individual children in isolation from other aspects of their work. We saw in Chapter 5 how some parents come to regard them not as allies in securing special provision for their child's education but as LEA officials seeking the solution most expedient for the LEA. An essential part of their work is to give LEA officers and schools informal advice on the education of children with learning or behavioural difficulties. In the sense that different individuals legitimately expect to receive a service from them, they have several 'clients': children, parents, teachers, LEA officers. These clients have different and often conflicting interests.

The amount of time spent on 1981 Act assessments varies from psychologist to psychologist and from LEA to LEA. A major influence, though, was the LEA's policy on accepting requests for assessment. This was important for two reasons: first, routine acceptance of virtually all requests, as happened in two LEAs, encouraged the belief among head teachers that this was the only way to obtain additional resources; second, it did nothing to encourage the informal assessment of children's needs advocated by the Warnock Report. Thus, psychologists who spent higher proportions of their time on formal assessment were more likely to find themselves negotiating with head teachers over resources, and less likely to be providing the accessible advice and support that class teachers might reasonably have expected.

What is assessed?

Given the variation between educational psychologists in other aspects of their work, at first sight there is an interesting consistency in their approach to assessment for the purposes of the 1981 Act. Standardised tests of intelligence and reading attainment were used in interviews with all but three of the children. Given the long-standing controversy within the profession over the use of IQ tests (e.g. Gillham, 1978) this is surprising; it is nevertheless consistent with DES (1989a) advice on assessments. There was less apparent agreement on the importance of understanding the wider context in which the child's problems were apparent.

In all cases but one, the child was interviewed by the psychologist. The exception was a teenager who had gone missing from home and the psychologist relied on a colleague's earlier report on the young person in preparing his advice for the LEA. Parents were also interviewed in every case.

Although most (93 per cent of cases) psychologists discussed the child's problems with the class teacher or, in a secondary school, head of year, form tutor or equivalent, only five children were observed by a psychologist in the classroom. Moreover, in spite of the clear evidence that teachers frequently attributed the child's behaviour in school to factors in the home background, only six families were visited at home. Even when psychologists clearly believed that home circumstances were the principal cause of the child's behavioural difficulties at school, and were intending to make a recommendation for residential schooling, the majority did not regard a home visit as a necessary part of their assessment. Personality assessment was carried out with only one child.

Choice of procedure

There was little consistency among psychologists as to why they used certain methods in preference to others. According to one:

There is a general problem with all clinical measures of social behaviour . . .

. how does one turn a response in a clinical situation to how one would actually respond in a real situation?

More important, for this psychologist, as for others in our study, test results were of secondary importance; they were not used principally to help reach a conclusion, but rather to support a judgement or to legitimise a conclusion that had been reached by other means. One psychologist hinted at this when he said:

I'm not necessarily using these factors (test results) in my judgements. They may be added information rather than the basis of the decision.

In practice, the job of the educational psychologist often focused quite explicitly on the management of conflict rather than on the clinical diagnosis of 'needs'. Thus, one psychologist observed:

Circumstances are very important and may vary between cases. It's not a matter of a psychologist deciding what emotional and behavioural difficulties are, and then using a set of criteria saying that this or that particular child has EBD. In practice, circumstances will define the complexity of the problem.

Thus, defining criteria for EBD was not a problem for this educational psychologist:

I find the Act very easy to work with because it does not ask me to define a problem, but rather to deal with it *as defined by the circumstances of the case*. I can describe an EBD child but I can't define one, nor do I need to do so. (Our *italics*)

This account gives an interesting insight into the role of educational psychologists and indicates that they must be responsive to a wide range of needs *besides* those of the individual child. The task of psychologists may be seen as managing the potentially conflicting needs and interests of different people in such a way that the child's educational opportunities are maximised. Thus, the criteria used in identifying emotional and behavioural difficulties can vary from case to case. This dispenses with the need to specify criteria which the *child* satisfies. Nevertheless, the notion of 'criteria' remains problematic. In practice, the focus of assessment was seldom the child's needs alone. The context within which those needs occurred, the contribution of school and family factors in the creation of the child's needs, and the needs and interests of others who came into contact with the child were all crucial elements which psychologists had to take into account in forming their professional judgements. Our observations and interviews suggested that assessment can best be conceptualised as a process of negotiation or conflict resolution. This is illustrated in the claim made by many teachers that the child was 'disturbed' (see Chapter 3).

Educational psychologists' reports

By the time we completed our fieldwork, educational psychologists' reports had been written on 22 of the 29 children. A decision had been made to discontinue the assessment of three children, and the assessment process had still not been completed for the remaining four. The reports we received varied both in length and in content. The majority contained evidence from psychometric and educational testing. Descriptions of the child's behaviour at school were more often based on second-hand information from teachers than on direct observation. Very few reports referred directly to strengths within the home and the school. Several, however, referred to factors within the home contributing to the child's behaviour patterns, though these were more often based on information from teachers or from parents in the course of an interview at school or at the psychologist's office than from discussion and observation gained on a home visit. In contrast, as noted in Chapter 3, no reports referred to contributory factors within the school. There were few attempts to suggest how the children's behaviour might be seen as a predictable result of interactions between factors in the children themselves – for example, health or temperament – and factors with the family, the school and the wider community. Nor was there much evidence in the reports we saw that children's views on the nature of their difficulties and on their future education had been sought and taken into account. Recommendations appeared to be aimed at LEA administrators rather than at the child's present or future teachers.

Table 6.1 summarises the principal sources of information that educational psychologists in our study used when making their assessments. Table 6.2 provides a content analysis of the 26 reports received. Two points should be made about these tables: first, they provide only a simple summary of a lengthy and often complex process; second, many educational psychologists explicitly stated at interview that they regarded their report as a necessary administrative formality, arguing that sensitive advice and guidance was best provided in the course of direct discussion with the parties involved. Both points raise important questions.

Parents clearly recognised the complexity of the process. As we argued in Chapter 5, however, they were at a disadvantage, lacking experience of the professional culture in which psychologists were working. This culture had built up over time, and reflected the aspects of the psychologists' work – for example, their wider role as LEA officers and their informal advisory work in schools. It is difficult to underestimate the power associated with access to this professional culture. It led to fundamental misperceptions which might have astonished and distressed the psychologists concerned, if they had been aware of them. For example, the parents of only five children said they were satisfied with the outcome of the assessment. Yet educational psychologists thought that parents of all but three of the 29 children were satisfied. Having been present at many of the psychologists' interviews with parents, we could readily understand *why* the psychologist thought the parents were satisfied. It was only after the event, in discussion with a researcher, that they became eloquent in expressing doubts and disquiet.

*Table 6.1 **Sources of information used by educational psychologists***

	Number of children N=29	Per cent of total
Interviews with head teachers	17	59
Interviews with class teachers, or (secondary school) form tutor, head of year or equivalent	27	93
Interview with parents	29	100
Interview with child	28	97
IQ test	26	87
Reading test	23	79
Personality test	1	3
Other diagnostic test	2	7
Home visit	17	59
Classroom observation	5	17

This was not because the interviews were conducted in an intimidating manner; rather it reflected the difficulty parents experienced in contributing to a process in which they were starting to learn 'rules' which psychologists had internalised over the course of their working lives. Like most 'rules' governing social interaction, they were assimilated rather than consciously learnt, and as a result the psychologists themselves were seldom fully aware of them. Superficially, it was easy to attribute misunderstandings to the unequal power relationship between psychologists and parents. Indeed, while writing the first draft of this chapter the author, a former educational psychologist, found himself referring to psychologists 'interviewing' parents and children but 'talking with' head teachers. Power relationships are deeply embedded in professional cultures, but it is an oversimplification to see them as the source of all tensions between professionals and clients.

Table 6.2 **Content analysis of educational psychologists' reports**

	Number of reports N=22	Per cent of total
Reference to intellectual assessment	20	91
Reference to reading test or other standardised educational assessment	17	77
Description of child's behaviour (based on second-hand information from teachers, parents, etc.)	20	91
Description of child's behaviour (based on direct observation)	9	41
Strengths within the home	0	0
Strengths within the school	2	9
Contributing factors with the home	12	54
Contributing factors within the school	0	0
Analysis of child's behaviour in terms of interaction between individual, family and school factors	1	4
Child's perception of own difficulties and/or future education	3	14
Parents' views on different possibilities for child's future education	2	9
Guidance for present/future teachers on educational management of child in the classroom	2	9

The hidden agenda in reports

To say that there was a hidden agenda in psychologists' reports is not to say that the individuals concerned were being in any way dishonest. Indeed, we frequently felt admiration for the way they grappled with peculiarly intransigent problems. Nevertheless, the nature of their task as LEA employees created a hidden agenda which could not fail to influence the content of their reports and the recommendations they contained. The agenda was 'hidden' only in the sense that parents would be likely to have difficulty in understanding the 'rules' governing report-writing. These rules form part of the assessment culture.

One such rule was that reports should not contain material which might reflect against the good name of the school or the LEA. To do so would be manifestly 'unprofessional'. Superficially this seems reasonable. Yet, as we saw in Table 3.1, it effectively prevents psychologists from drawing attention to factors in school or classroom organisation which might have contributed to the child's difficulties.

Less obviously, although most psychologists used tests of intelligence and reading attainment (Table 6.1), the results of these seldom played a major part in their recommendations. No children were referred for special education because of the results of psychometric assessment, though it is certainly true that if the tests had revealed more serious cognitive or educational problems, as happened in one case, a different recommendation might have been made. In this sense, psychometric assessment could be seen as a screening procedure. In discussion with us, many educational psychologists clearly recognised that testing was often used to legitimise a decision, rather than to assist in reaching it. Thus, if other factors, such as the child's exclusion from school, were exerting pressure for referral to a special school, or for additional resources in the mainstream, the test results could be used to justify the recommendation.

For parents, however, there was a further problem. In their discussions with parents, psychologists frequently acknowledged the 'real' problems arising from the child's adjustment at school. In these discussions, psychologists could be very open in recognising tensions within the school. They could also be very open about the limitations the LEA could offer. They seldom talked about the results of intelligence and reading tests, since these were marginal not only to the parents' concerns but also to the eventual decision. Thus, when parents received the psychologist's report and read, for the first time, about the detailed testing their child had undergone, they felt bewildered and resentful. Their bewilderment at the prominence given to psychometric testing was matched only by their resentment that no mention was made of the crucial issues they had discussed face-to-face with the psychologist. Yet for the psychologist, to put *these* issues in a report would have been the height of folly – insensitive and undiplomatic towards teacher and LEA colleagues at best, and at worst thoroughly 'unprofessional'.

Role conflict

The Association of Educational Psychologists' Code of Professional Practice states that:

The Educational Psychologist aims to protect the welfare of any person who may seek his [sic] service or be the subject of his study. He does not use his professional position or relationships, nor does he knowingly permit his services or knowledge to be used by others, for purposes inconsistent with this general aim. (AEP, 1984, p. 20)

We were not aware of any of the educational psychologists in our study disputing this general aim in their work. Without exception, they saw themselves as providing a service to children and their families. Yet they *also* saw themselves as providing a service to schools, and in discussions with the researchers they recognised the tension this could create. Head teachers generally had clear expectations regarding the outcome of a child's assessment. Similarly, LEA officers responsible for the allocation of resources looked to psychologists for advice in their decision-making. Whatever their personal views, it was inconceivable that psychologists could 'protect the welfare' of children referred to them without in any way being affected by the legitimate expectations of other professional colleagues.

Professional relationships and priorities

In their review of educational psychology services in England, DES, HMI (1990) noted that 'there are strong pressures on psychologists to work with individual children and this remains central to their role' (para. 4). Yet they also reported that

in some schools psychologists are regarded mainly as the key to additional resources or the removal of a pupil. In these cases it is difficult for individual psychologists to work in the child's best interests with the school, and although such instances were in the minority, cases were observed where decisions had been unduly influenced by the negative attitudes of the mainstream school staff. (para. 40)

HMI's observations illustrate the ambiguities in the role of educational psychologists and point towards the ethical dilemmas that may consequently confront them. Parents and teachers expect educational psychologists to work with individual children. This, after all, is one of their main functions. Yet teachers also see psychologists as the key to increased resources. So, from a quiet different perspective, do LEA administrators. These conflicting expectations often result in confusion as to who is the psychologist's principal 'client'.

In their contribution to this debate, Dupont and Dowdney (1990a, b) describe how a clinical psychologist is consulted by Jeremy's mother at the suggestion of his school because of the latter's concern over his disruptive behaviour in school. At this point Jeremy and his mother are identified by the psychologist as his clients. However, following an assessment of the situation, the psychologist forms the opinion that circumstances within the school are the source of Jeremy's difficulties. Therefore the psychologist considers it is the school and not the child who should now be the real client. Yet 'to address the school as a client would involve a change of role – moving away from direct intervention at the level of the individual pupil to a more general consultative role' (Dupont and Dowdney, 1990a, p. 114).

According to Dupont and Dowdney, this would not be possible

unless the teachers consented. Without the willingness of the teachers to become the psychologist's client it would be unethical to attempt to carry out the consultation (Dupont and Dowdney, 1990b). They rejected Galloway's (1990b) argument – namely, that if the LEA 'asked them to intervene within the school they were ethically entitled to attempt to do so, whether the staff were enthusiastic or not' (p. 40). In rejecting this solution they appear to be confusing the ethical justification for a course of action with a pragmatic assessment of its chances of success. Clearly, successful intervention is unlikely if teachers are unwilling to cooperate. The same applies to consultation, which we would regard as a special form of intervention. Just as clearly, until their responsibility to inspect schools was removed by the 1991 Education Act, LEAs had a legal and moral duty to intervene if a child's education was suffering owing to the pressures teachers felt themselves to be facing. Indeed, it was precisely when a school's staff was most reluctant to accept the need to review the effectiveness of their work that the LEA's duty to intervene was most obvious, as the Auld Report on William Tynedale School made clear (ILEA, 1976). The ethical basis for professional action should not be confused with the very real practical problems facing professionals when they have decided the form of intervention that is most appropriate.

This case does, however, illustrate the ethical problems that can arise when several different people see themselves as a psychologist's client. These problems become particularly acute when the psychologist also implicitly regards different people as his or her client, and these people have conflicting interests. We explore these issues in relation to Dupont and Dowdney's case, and further illustrate the complexity of pressures on psychologists from case histories in our own research.

Whose client?

The referral of Jeremy to the clinical psychologist was made by his mother. Jeremy and his mother were, therefore, the psychologist's clients. The fact that the school suggested the referral to Jeremy's mother makes no difference. However, the school implicitly also saw itself as the client:

The class teacher and head teacher were anxious for a clinical psychology input and requested that a behaviour programme be designed to help moderate Jeremy's behaviour. (Dupont and Dowdney, 1990a, p. 13)

The client status of the school was implicitly accepted by the psychologist because, in response to this request, he undertook a full functional analysis. This examines the child's behaviour, 'but also considers the social structures of which the child is part' (p. 13). The psychologist recognised that 'such analyses may well highlight the need for changes within the family or school as a prerequisite for behavioural change in the child' (p. 13). Thus, this assessment quite clearly saw both Jeremy and the school as potential clients. This created no dilemmas until the conclusion was drawn that Jeremy's behaviour was the product of classroom organisation and management and related factors. Even then, it only created a problem when the school did not accept this formulation. When the child was perceived as the primary client, the psychologist's role was conceptualised in terms of meeting Jeremy's needs within the framework of school expectations. When, following an empirical investigation of Jeremy's needs within this framework, the initial conceptualisation was no longer tenable, conceptualisation of the psychologist's role changed, with the school becoming the primary client. That the psychologist could make this shift illustrates the scope for exercise of professional judgements. Nevertheless, it also illustrates how the demands of different individuals who expect some kind of service from psychologists may influence the latter's perception of their own role.

In Jeremy's case, the psychologist's method of assessment implicitly recognised the teachers as potential clients. It is relevant to note here that clients who are also professional colleagues may feel themselves to have different, implicitly higher, status in relation to the psychologist than clients who are not. Moreover, if the role of psychologists is defined in terms of responding to individual referrals, this may combine with their beliefs about 'professional' behaviour permitting or prohibiting criticism of colleagues, to influence their interpretation of the available evidence. The point is that educational and clinical child psychologists expect to receive referrals from teachers, but the problems these referrals present may result, at least in part, from problems in their schools.

There is a danger here of adopting double standards. Identifying contributory factors in the child and/or the family presents no professional problem. Yet identifying contributory factors in the school leaves one open to the charge of unhelpful or even 'unprofessional' criticism and, as Dupont and Dowdney (1990b) quite legitimately point out, may result in 'opening up the possibility that children who did need help would remain unreferred' (p. 15).

Thus an apparently straightforward referral can create ethical and professional pressures. Not only do these pressures constrain the action available to psychologists, they also encourage particular ways of conceptualising the problem. In Jeremy's case, the school, through his mother, dictated the terms of the referral, thereby implicitly claiming the right to contribute to a definition of the problem in terms of Jeremy being a difficult child who needed to be taught to behave differently. Yet by responding to the school's perception of Jeremy, irrespective of whether he agreed with it, a psychologist would be in danger of reinforcing the focus on Jeremy as a problem child. The ethical dilemma for psychologists, therefore, is deeply rooted in the professional ambiguity of their role. It arises largely from the different and competing claims to 'client status' made by participants with different perceptions of the psychologist's role.

Schools contain within them a multiplicity of interacting, interdependent and occasionally conflicting needs. Within a school, as we have seen, identification of the child as client may, despite being consistent with the ethical codes of professional associations, nonetheless involve professional dilemmas for the psychologist. In practice, psychologists acknowledge responsibilities extending beyond the needs of individual children. These responsibilities are to the LEA or health service as their employer, and to the school for whom they provide a service. In our research, educational psychologists recognised the potential for conflict that may arise from these divided loyalties. Aware that different clients might have different interests and needs, some psychologists understood their role as one of facilitating consensus or managing conflict. To quote one educational psychologist:

The major client is the child but it is necessary to look at the wider context . . . to take account of the needs of teachers and other children . . . sometimes teachers fall out with psychologists because they think we're not concerned with their needs.

In another case the school was strongly requesting a child's transfer to a special school. Although the child had temporarily been excluded, the psychologist thought this was inappropriate. His solution was to play for time. He recommended a return to mainstream school, with a behavioural contract drawn up between the child, teachers, parents and himself. However, the school was only prepared to accept this proposal on condition that a Statement be prepared under provision in the 1981 Education Act, specifying special schooling if a further trial within the mainstream proved unsuccessful.

On the occasions when parental wishes and the psychologist's perception of the child's interests come into conflict with the LEA and/or school, the tensions inherent in the psychologist's role are particularly evident. Once again, what is significant in creating this tension is not so much the psychologist's perception of his or her role as the perceptions others have of that role.

Models of professional–client relationship: complementary or conflicting?

The differences between clients and fellow professionals in their perceptions of the psychologist's role reflect the model of the professional relationship they each expect. At least five models are familiar to most psychologists, psychiatrists and social workers.

1. *The 'doctor–patient' model.* The professional is seen as an expert who will make a diagnosis or assessment of the presenting problem and provide treatment.
2. *The 'advocacy' model.* The professional acts as advocate in support of a client – for example, over a housing problem or a conflict with school or LEA. This model could include helping children in care exercise their rights under the 1981 Education Act.
3. *The 'consultancy' model.* This often overlaps with the advocacy model. As in that model, there is no expectation that treatment should be provided. The professional offers expert information or advice. This may be sought by parents or, less frequently, by children. It may also be sought by the courts or some other organisation with a legitimate interest in the case.
4. *The 'child protection' model.* This includes investigating and advising on cases of suspected child abuse, or taking action on abuse when it is discovered in the course of other interventions.
5. *The 'resource management' model.* The professionals' principal task is to give their employing authority advice which will assist in allocating resources.

Most professionals have experience of working with each model. They also, incidentally, have had experience of each model when they themselves have been clients or patients. Only at the most superficial level, however, are the five models discrete. Advocacy and child protection overlap in obvious ways, as do the doctor–patient and consultancy models. Indeed, the closer one looks, the more evident it becomes that any professional's perception of the nature of a professional relationship, and hence of the appropriate model, can vary from session to session.

A more serious difficulty, however, is that clients can differ in their perceptions of the professional's role, and their perceptions may conflict with the professional's own perception of it. As we have seen, different individuals may consider themselves to be a psychologist's client in the sense of having a legitimate expectation that the psychologist will provide them with a service. At such times, conflict and/or confusion can be difficult to avoid. This is illustrated by an educational psychologist's assessment of Ben, who we first met in Chapter 5 (p. 73). Ben's parents, the head of an off-site unit he had been attending for four days each week and the educational psychologist all felt strongly that he should be fully integrated into a mainstream primary school before reaching secondary school age. The primary school was willing to admit Ben, but only on condition that additional resources were provided. The LEA thought this condition inappropriate:

besides the heavy demand this would place on scarce resources, it could be argued that if special resources, so much in excess of the normal provision in a mainstream school, are required to make reintegration feasible, then the child is not yet ready for reintegration.

Thus, in this case the parents initially perceived themselves and Ben to be the psychologist's clients. They wanted Ben to be reintegrated into the mainstream and relied upon the psychologist to help achieve this goal. In other words, they expected an advocacy model of intervention. However, they eventually started to doubt whether he would act in Ben's interests rather than the authority's. Thus, they suggested he was now working within a resource management model.

From the host school's perspective it was the client. The teachers saw the role of the psychologist as being to secure resources for their use in return for accepting a 'difficult' child: 'Extra support full time. That is the only condition on which we would take him'.

The educational psychologist was very responsive to this view, accepting that ' there is no professional formula (for identifying EBD). It's a matter of satisfying the school's needs, not the child's.' Here, the school saw the psychologist as an advocate who would help secure additional resources.

The LEA saw the psychologist's role as a consultant providing them with advice which they could then use as a basis for their own decision-making and the efficient management of resources. Yet the educational psychologist's role in decision-making within this authority was a particular source of tension. According to the educational psychologist, when he started to write the 'Proposed Statement' of Ben's special educational needs, he was acting as an LEA administrator, and hence a resource manager, not as a psychologist.

. . . when I put down my psychological advice and pick up my draft Statement I cease to be a psychologist and become an administrator. . . . I find this swapping of hats a difficult business.

The conflicting perceptions that these 'clients' had of the psychologist's role led the psychologist towards potential conflict with all of them. Conflict with the LEA was possible if he chose to attempt to use the Statementing procedures as a way of obtaining resources that the LEA had previously refused to make available. Conflict with parents was already occurring since they were suspicious about his role as an LEA officer and the implications that this might have for the outcome of assessment. They recognised that Ben was approaching secondary transfer age and at that time a Statement would be necessary if he were to be placed in a special school. They were deeply concerned that this might be the outcome of the assessment and did not accept the psychologist's view of himself as an advocate on their behalf. Conflict with the school was also likely since the head was unhappy with the psychologist's failure to deliver the level of support he desired despite his staff's own sense of goodwill. The psychologist was aware that he was concerned with the management of conflict. However, he was the focus of the conflict. His loyalties were divided by the different and conflicting expectations of his 'clients'.

Decision-making in professional practice

By now it should be clear that assessment is not a simple information-gathering exercise from which logical and agreed recommendations inevitably emerge. As in all social interactions, participants have to 'make sense' of the information they receive, as well as deciding what additional information to seek. Again, as in all social interaction, they attempt to influence each other's perception of the nature of the problem. We have argued that lack of prior experience and involvement in a professional culture places parents and children at a disadvantage compared with educational psychologists and other professionals.

Very often the choice of interview location itself (and who makes that choice) is undertaken with a particular purpose in mind. In one interview we observed, the education offices were chosen by the psychologist as the location for an interview with a child who had been expelled from school. The reason given for this choice was that they 'offered neutral territory'. In another case the psychologist saw parents in their own home because it was felt they would be 'likely to feel more relaxed on home ground' and therefore more freely communicative. On yet another occasion the psychologist preferred the more formal setting of 'the office', 'with a desk between us' because the child 'knows then that this is a formal assessment and not just a friendly chat'. The location of each interview was a method of indicating to the interviewee what the interviewer's expectations of the interview were. Similarly, the interviewer was concerned to establish these meanings within the interviewee's own perception of the interview's purpose. The interviewee could, of course, make choices about the interview location in order to establish the interviewer's expectations of roles, status, etc., in precisely the same way, although the authority and status embedded in professional roles could make that difficult for parents. In one case in our study, where a parent wished to make some 'serious allegations' concerning the way her child had been dealt with by one of the professionals, her insistence that the psychologist visit her home was intended to reinforce her view that the latter was her adviser and advocate.

Where the interviewer has attempted to define the expectations of the interviewee it remains the case that the interviewee may interpret this information in quite different ways from those intended. For instance, in one case the psychologist arranged a meeting with a parent in school because he believed the parent had a positive relationship with the school. The parent did indeed share a similar belief; nonetheless, she found the prospect of an interview with the psychologist at school to be a source of great anxiety: 'I thought he (her son) was in bother at school.' Moreover, the parent's sense of powerlessness was reinforced by the circumstances of the invitation to attend the interview:

The biggest shock was that there was a letter behind the door from Mrs Blake (head teacher) to say that Mr. Sandford (EP) wanted to see me at 2.30 pm and it was 3.30 pm when I got in.

The precise implications of decisions about interview locations vary from case to case, and these implications cannot be anticipated by adopting any set formula. In practice, convenience dictates that much of an educational psychologist's work will be carried out in the setting of the child's school. Our data supports an interactionist perspective, suggesting that in planning and conducting an interview it is important to consider: (a) the relationship between purpose and location; (b) how this is actually perceived by the interviewee; and (c) the effect of such perceptions on the information elicited by the interview (see the discussion of interviews with children in Tammivaara and Enright (1986)).

The location and setting of an initial meeting between an educational psychologist and parent or child can be seen as just one stage in a complex process of negotiation involving many actors. Before reaching the decision to seek a formal assessment, head teachers in our study had had extensive discussions with the children's class teachers. These, too, can be seen as a process of establishing a shared view of the nature of the problem. They formed part of the framework within which the psychologist would have to work. They also served to influence the future course of events. Whatever views the psychologists might form from interviews with children and their parents, these would have to be negotiated not only with children and parents but also with teachers and, if additional resources were required, with LEA administrators. If, as in Dupont and Dowdney's (1990a) case of Jeremy, and that of Ben in our own research, assessment of the child reveals shortcomings in the school or in the LEA's resources, psychologists almost inevitably find themselves at the centre of conflict.

Conclusions

In Chapters 4 and 5 we identified some of the dilemmas facing children and their parents in the course of an assessment of special educational needs. Clearly 'undergoing assessment', or 'being assessed', is an entirely different matter from 'taking part' in assessments. Yet assessment is a social process with social as well as educational consequences for the children concerned. If children and their parents cannot take part in the process, with all the implications that this implies for their ability to influence the course of events, frustration, resentment and feeling of inadequacy are the predictable results. In this chapter, however, we have shown that the process is neither easier nor more comfortable for educational psychologists.

Although their training and experience appear to place them at the heart of the process, there are powerful constraints on their freedom to serve the children and parents who constitute their primary clients. They also have to provide a service to schools and to LEA administrators, and the legitimate expectations of these secondary 'clients' provide the context within which they work. Even if they were able to offer an entirely independent service, free from any obligation to schools and to their employing LEA, educational psychologists might still face a dilemma over the model of professional relationships to adopt at any given time. A consultancy model can merge with advocacy and lead to a 'doctor–patient' relationship or to a child protection role. The relationship can vary from session to session and even within a session.

If educational psychologists were only accountable to children and parents, the nature of their role might perhaps be negotiated and clarified without undue difficulty. The reality is that they are caught in a complex web in which the interests of their secondary clients, namely teachers and other LEA officers, are dictated by wider considerations arising from muddle and confusion in government policy. The problem is illustrated by the discourses of need outlined in Chapter 1. The 1981 Act is based on the 'special needs child' discourse; children's individual needs must be identified, and resources provided to meet them. In practice, if not in theory, the adequacy of existing arrangements does not form part of the assessment. In contrast, the 1988 Education Reform Act and subsequent legislation is based on the 'school failure' discourse. Learning and, to a lesser extent, behavioural difficulties are seen as the result of inadequate teaching. The government's quite explicit aim was to impose changes which would raise standards without providing major additional resources; the solution to the problems of low- and/or under-achievement lay in reforming the school system, not in providing additional bits and pieces which would leave the main structure unchanged.

Not surprisingly, head teachers have resented this analysis. At the same time, parents have been becoming increasingly well informed and, as a further result of government policy, more effective in their determination to secure the best possible educational provisions for their children. The result is predictable. The number of children referred for assessment of their special educational needs has increased. So has the number of children excluded from school for difficult behaviour. As external pressures on teachers have increased, so have pressures on LEAs to provide additional resources for problem pupils. LEAs have been faced with an increasing demand on a static resource. They look to their educational psychologists for a way out of this *impasse*. The psychologists have no solution. Their professional training as clinicians or as specialists in learning and behavioural difficulties has become increasingly irrelevant. Instead, their time and skills are spent in a tortuous process of arbitration and negotiation which, at best, can succeed in pacifying a majority of their clients while satisfying few of them. They should not be criticised too strongly for failing to resolve ambiguities and contradictions arising from the structure within which they work.

PART III

Looking beyond the data

CHAPTER 7

Categories and social identities

Introduction

In Chapters 1–3 we examined the concept of special educational needs and the legislative framework within which special provision can be made in England and Wales. We argued that the concept is confused on a number of counts. 'Special' needs may be a normal response to abnormal conditions. 'Educational' needs may have more to do with the social climate of the playground than the curriculum. It is not even clear whether the 'needs' being addressed are those of children with learning and behavioural problems who are referred for assessment, or those of teachers who, perhaps legitimately, are concerned about *other* children and about their own stress levels.

In Chapters 4–6 we analysed some of the tensions, dilemmas and contradictions arising from the assessment process as constituted in the 1981 and 1993 Education Acts. We argued that the motive behind referral was seldom, if ever, to determine whether a child has special educational needs, but to secure a particular outcome: the child's removal from school, additional resources, or an undertaking to act rapidly if matters deteriorated. Educational psychologists regarded children and parents as their primary clients, but recognised that they must maintain a working relationship with the schools at which they are expected to provide a service. They also recognised the finite nature of LEA resources. Parents and many children gradually became aware of this hidden agenda. In consequence, the principal function of assessment was to negotiate solutions that were as acceptable as possible to everyone concerned.

Special education provides more problematic categories, labels and identities than any other part of the education system, most of them carrying a stigma of inferiority, low status, or deviance from some acceptable norm. To be labelled as a child with emotional and behavioural difficulties carries particularly negative connotations. To acquire this identity has profound consequences for the young person concerned, in terms of future education, employment possibilities and life chances. This chapter discusses the social consequences of the assessment and categorisation of children, the development of the categories of special education, and the way in which children

regarded as deviating from norms of acceptable behaviour come to
acquire the social identity of being emotionally and behaviourally
disturbed.

Who Benefits?

From the point of view of most practitioners and professionals
involved in the assessment of children with 'special educational
needs', the process is rational and humane, and is designed to help
individual children. The ideology that Tomlinson (1982) termed
benevolent humanitarianism is still very strong, along with the
assumption that special education provision is an enlightened, logical
and moral response to individuals who 'have problems' and who are
assumed to benefit by the assessment.

Over the past decade the belief that assessing and labelling more
and more children as having special educational needs is a purely
objective, scientific and humanitarian process has been subjected to
much criticism, especially in the UK, the USA and Australia (see
Barton and Tomlinson, 1984; Fulcher, 1989; Galloway and Goodwin,
1987; Sigmon, 1987; Tomlinson, 1982; Ysseldyke and Algozzine,
1982). There is now a much greater awareness that the labels and
categories of special education, developed as they have been at
particular historical times, are social constructions which do not
necessarily have any intrinsic meaning. Fulcher, examining special
education assessment in Europe, the USA and Australia, has pointed
out that in all these countries complex processes have been developed
to produce 'special identities' for large numbers of children. For the
majority of children who acquire such an identity, however, 'no known
impairment exists' (Fulcher, 1989, p. 25). It is often the subjective
judgements, based on the beliefs, interests and needs of those who do
the labelling, which are as important as any characteristics imputed to
those who are given a label and a subsequent social identity. There is
also a much greater awareness now of the social consequences for
children who are educated as 'special'. The economic recession in
Britain has made it more obvious that to have received a special
education, even a non-statemented special education in an integrated
setting, is likely to be regarded unfavourably by many employers.

Critics of labels and categories have also come in for criticism.
Norwich (1990) has argued that those who object to the labels of
special education are social egalitarians and that differentiation in
educational provision does not necessarily imply differences in
personal and social value, and Soder (1992) points out that
'non-labelling' does not necessarily change the social situation of the
individuals. It is still the case, however, that to acquire a 'special'
label, whether statutory or non-statutory, and be offered differential
educational provision on the basis of this label, does affect the way

individuals are socially valued, and it crucially affects their perception of their own identity. The labels and categories of special education do not necessarily benefit the children, but they do benefit the whole education system and the wider society.

It was not surprising, in the study reported in this book, to find that it was classroom teachers who made initial requests for children to be assessed, having already concluded that they 'had EBD'. Understandably, the teachers were sometimes more concerned with the beneficial effects for their classrooms if the children whose behaviour they regarded as unacceptable, were removed, than in questioning the epistemological status of the concept of EBD. One head explained:

If we try to fit in with individual children we get pressure from (other) parents to move their children. That's what happened in this case. I've had parents coming in to complain about what he's done – disrupting other children's work.

Another head was more explicit:

An exclusion is the only answer sometimes, to get things shifting, and you have to think of (other) kids and the staff.

Classroom teachers undoubtedly benefit from the removal of troublesome children from their classrooms. The 1921 Education Act led to those children who were 'anti-social or a nuisance' being the most likely candidates for removal, after 'certification' to special schools or classes (Cameron, 1931) and this situation continues at the present time. Teachers are constrained, by the nature of the organisation they work in, to participate in the assessment processes which produce the special child, and help construct social identities for pupils which may have long-term detrimental social consequences for the child. As one teacher explained:

He distracts other children. He disturbs their work. I have to move other children in the class around frequently, so that they don't have to tolerate him for too long. . . . You see, all the time he has difficulty in conforming to the rules of the school. We have to keep strict rules.

It must be recognised that an education system which has developed mechanisms for removing troublesome pupils, or at least for minimising their influence, has benefited enormously. Educators in such a system are able to concentrate on the meritocratic education of the able and the conforming, unimpeded by the undoubted problems that arise when difficult children remain in ordinary classrooms, and there is no necessity for the school system or organisation to change. The wider society also benefits from any certification or statementing which validates the removal or special treatment of these children, in that it has been given advance warning that particular individuals may pose problems for authority later in their lives.

The origins of categories

The origins of the statutory categories of handicap, disability or special educational needs lie in the development of mass education systems which necessitated the recognition of pupils who could not function satisfactorily within the system and interfered with its smooth running. How to define such pupils has always posed a problem, and the changing terminology of defect, disability, handicap, and special needs is an indication that such terms are social constructs developed within particular historical contexts. The 1886 Idiots Act provided a good example of the circularity of some of the assessment criteria which led to individuals acquiring a particular identity. 'Idiocy', the Act declared, 'means a greater deficiency of intellect, and imbecility means a lesser degree of such deficiency.' The Egerton Commission, which reported in 1889, was particularly concerned with children variously designated as feeble-minded, educable imbeciles and the badly behaved. It was children thus described who formed the clientele of the first special schools set up in large cities in the 1890s. Other schools set up standard 0 classes for children who could not reach the required standard of what would now be called test performance. These classes were necessary because of the large number of pupils with learning and behaviour problems. A London school inspector noted in 1897 that 'out of every seventy children, twenty-five were entirely ignorant, they misbehaved, learned nothing and truanted' (Pritchard, 1963, p. 117). Thus, a Victorian statistic was that 35 per cent of children impeded the smooth running of mainstream schools. Eighty years later the percentage was variously considered to be 20 per cent by the Warnock Committee (DES, 1978), 40 per cent by Keith Joseph when Secretary of State for Education in 1982, and even 50 per cent by the Scottish Education Department (SED, 1978).

The need to remove troublesome children from mainstream schools and classes was also evident in the USA, where compulsory school attendance brought into schools large numbers of 'retarded, rebellious and deviant pupils' who disrupted the education of others. A teacher in a New York school in the 1890s described her ungraded class as 'not the result of any educational theory, but simply the odds and ends of a large school, – naughty, dull and stupid children' (Lazarson, 1983, p. 20).

Yet even in the nineteenth century there was no unambiguous acceptance that it was qualities within children that necessitated their labelling or differential treatment outside mainstream schools. A London inspector in the 1890s considered that 'dull and naughty children were manufactured by the cast-iron requirements of modern education codes' (Barrett, 1986, p. 188). This is a view that has received more recent attention, for example, by Skrtic (1991) who graphically explained the way in which non-acceptable pupils who cannot be 'squeezed into' what is regarded as normal school organisation must be 'squeezed out' rather than the organisation changing to adapt to the pupils.

Statutory categories of handicap continued to expand during the twentieth century, and more and more children had quite distinct and stigmatised social identities bestowed on them, and were treated differentially within an expanding subsystem of special education. Table 7.1 illustrates the expansion of statutory categories of 'handicap' between 1886 and 1981, and the descriptive categories used in the period since the 1981 Special Education Act. Children and young people who were assessed and placed in any particular category acquired a particular but stigmatised social identity. Over the period 1920–93 a variety of interest groups lobbied for an expansion of categories, some of which are also listed in Table 7.1. The suggested 'neuropathic' child of the 1920s was, for example, a precursor of the maladjusted child. By 1978 it is was obvious that there could be no indefinite expansion of categories, since resources would not allow this, and the Warnock Committee recommended the abolition of categories of handicap (DES, 1978). However, post-1981, descriptive labels for children continued to proliferate and behaviours continued to be ascribed to children once they had been placed in a category: 'he's like that because he is epileptic, dyslexic, emotionally disturbed'. What is interesting about the categories, whether statutory or descriptive, is that they constitute a mix of supposed genetic, environmental, developmental and behavioural assumptions.

In terms of numbers it has always been these children who are now considered to have mild or moderate learning difficulties or emotional and behavioural problems who constitute the largest groups. Children who pre-war were categorised as feeble-minded, or educable defective were post-war termed the educationally subnormal, and children who had been variously described as nervous, difficult, neuropathic, antisocial or moral defective became a statutory category of maladjusted pupil. Squibb (1981, p. 47) worked out that between 1960 and 1976 numbers in the category of ESN increased by 237 per cent and in the maladjusted category by 150 per cent. He suggested that by increasing the structural processes set up to deal with those considered deviant, the numbers of deviant children increases. Certainly, the notion that there is an expanding number of pupils with learning and behavioural problems, whose presence, or even absence by truancy, is troublesome to ordinary schools, has become a well-established truism of the twentieth century.

TABLE 7.1 Categories of handicap: 1886–Post-1981

Statutory categories					Descriptive categories		Some suggested categories 1920–93 never formally adopted
1886	1899	1913	1945	1970	Post-1981	1920–93
Idiot	Idiot	Idiot	Severely sub-normal (SSN)	Educationally sub-normal severe (ESN-S)	Child with learning difficulty (severe)	Neuropathic
Imbecile	Imbecile (educable imbecile, feeble-minded)	Imbecile			Profoundly handicapped	Nervous
		Moral imbecile (moral defective)				Psychiatrically crippled
						Aphasic
	Blind	Blind	Blind	Blind	Visually impaired	Clumsy
			Partially sighted	Partially sighted		Hyperactive/Hyperkinetic
	Deaf	Deaf	Deaf	Deaf	Hearing impaired	Severely lethargic
			Partially deaf	Partially Deaf		
	Epileptic	Epileptic	Epileptic	Epileptic		Inconsequential
	Defective	Mental defective (feeble minded)	Educationally sub-normal (ESN)	Educationally sub-normal moderate (ESN-M)	Child with learning difficulty (mild or moderate)	Additive-influenced
						Attention-span deficit
						Augmentative communication problem
			Maladjusted	Maladjusted	Emotionally and behaviourally disturbed (EBD)	Behavioural, emotional and social problem (BESP)
		Physical defective	Physically handicapped	Physically handicapped	Physically handicapped	Socially handicapped
					Disabled	
			Speech defect	Speech defect	Speech defect	Specific learning difficulty (SpLD)
			Delicate	Delicate		Challenging behaviour
			Diabetic	Dyslexic[1]		
				Autistic[1]		

The origins of the EBD child

Children who exhibit behaviour that is deemed to be deviant from prevailing norms of good conduct have always been regarded as a social problem.

Hurt (1988) has recorded that under a Poor Law Act of 1597 a large number of 'ill-disposed children of whom the City of London is desirous to be disemburdened' were sent to the American colonies as servants. Prior to compulsory education, vagrant, delinquent and pauper children were usually dealt with by being dispatched to workhouse schools, reformatories, industrial schools or 'ragged' schools. Unsurprisingly, they were overwhelmingly the children of the poor and dispossessed whose parents had often been judged to be socially undesirable. Lord Shaftesbury noted in 1848 that of pupils in 15 ragged schools '162 had been in prison, 116 had run away from home because of ill-treatment, 170 had slept in lodging houses, 253 lived by begging, 216 had no shoes, 68 were the children of convicts, 219 had never slept in beds, and 306 had lost one or both parents' (Ford *et al.*, 1982, p. 39).

The eugenics movement, which was most influential in the early twentieth century, assumed that the lower social classes were most likely to produce defective and disruptive children, who would subsequently endanger society, and their defects were linked to moral depravity, pauperism, crime, prostitution and unemployment. Political interest in the social control of potentially disruptive children was therefore paramount, and politicians looked to the medical profession and the emerging profession of educational psychologists to identify, assess and treat the symptoms, if not the causes, of deviant and disruptive behaviour. Ford *et al.* (1982, p. 39) have pointed out that

towards the end of the nineteenth century the disciplines of medicine and psychology were equipping themselves with insights and techniques which the Boards of Education would consider useful in dealing with a variety of school problems, including disruption.

Disruptive pupils were originally often classified with those with learning problems as educable imbeciles, feeble-minded, mentally defective and later ESN. The 1913 Mental Deficiency Act created a category of moral imbeciles or defectives, and children who displayed emotionally disturbed or disruptive behaviour came to be associated with both mental defect and moral defect.

The category of maladjusted which emerged in the 1945 Handicapped Pupils and School Health Regulations, thus had its origins in the early labels of moral and mental defect, the neuropathic, unstable, nervous and difficult children noted in Board of Education reports during the 1920s and in the 'difficult and maladjusted child' recommended in the 1929 Board of Education report as in need of child guidance. Associations with the category were at best those of personal deficiencies and inadequacies, and at worst with moral depravity and a variety of social evils. Thus, the social identity of any child assessed post-1944 as maladjusted, and later as emotionally and behaviourally disturbed, is one which has a powerful history of stigma, being associated with undesirable personal and social characteristics.

The construction of the EBD child

Attempts to define more clearly the characteristics of the maladjusted or disruptive child have been regularly attempted since 1944. The assumption made is that the problems lie within the individual child but the major concern is with the effect of the child's behaviour on other pupils, teachers and classrooms. The Underwood Committee (MoE, 1955) which was given the task of reporting on the 'medical, social and educational problems of the maladjusted child', identified six sets of within-child symptoms – professional action by educational psychologists and child guidance clinics being required to alleviate all these. The Warnock Committee (DES, 1978) recommended that children with 'severe emotional and behavioural disorders' should be sent to special schools, but did not define severe EBD. Numbers of pupils ascertained as maladjusted under the 1944 Act rose sharply during the 1960s and 1970s, as did those assessed as ESN, teachers often using this latter category to refer disruptive pupils, and there was a dramatic increase in non-statutory forms of provision for children who posed problems for ordinary classrooms. Behavioural units, withdrawal and guidance centres, nurture groups, tutorial classes and various other places, were all used to remove troublesome and disruptive pupils speedily from mainstream classes, but there has never been a consensus as to either the causes or the symptoms of disruption. Galloway and Goodwin concluded in 1987 that 'the common point to emerge from attempts to clarify behavioural disorders and types of maladjustment is that it is a ragbag term describing any kind of behaviour that teachers and parents find disturbing' (Galloway and Goodwin, 1987, p. 32).

It is unsurprising that there has never been a consensus on 'what is' an EBD child. As a descriptive category it is non-normative (Tomlinson, 1982; Cooper *et al.*, 1991), that is, it relies on the subjective judgements of teachers and other professionals rather than on any agreed objective criteria. The nearest professionals come to agreement is that while a child's behaviour may be both disturbed and disturbing (Galloway and Goodwin, 1987), there are likely to be psychological or medical factors associated with the behaviour. Thus, Lord Elton's report on *Discipline in Schools* (DES, 1989b) defines a child with emotional and behavioural difficulties as one with 'severe and persistent behaviour problems as a result of emotional, psychological or neurological disturbance' (para. 6:29). This is an indication that the medico-psychological model, established by early twentieth-century medical and psychological control of assessment procedures for special education, is still dominant, rather than any theory of interpersonal or social interaction or of school participation in the development of deviant or disruptive behaviour.

The application of a medical model to children whose behaviour is irritating to others has been subjected to stringent criticisms from Ford *et al*., (1982) who argue that the concept of 'illness' implies an understanding of the cause and cure for the behaviour. Using medical analogies strengthens the belief that the source of the problems of disruptive behaviour lies in the child rather than in interaction between the child and others, or as a child's rational reaction to difficult situations. Ford and her colleagues point out that the enduring popularity of pseudo-medical explanations for EBD is related to the relief many parents and teachers feel on being offered explanations for a child's behaviour which does not constitute a moral judgement on them. Thus, parents may feel absolved from feeling that they have been 'bad' parents and may even join in victimising their child. Teachers may feel absolved from considering whether their own behaviour or reactions initiate disruptive behaviour, and they can feel satisfactorily 'caring' when they refer a child for expert help.

There was certainly some evidence of these kinds of feelings in our study. Some of the children were able to consider whether they were being blamed for being 'ill' or 'wrong' when their behaviour was a logical result of poor interpersonal relationships between adults. One boy who believed his assessment was initiated because he had difficulties with his mother told us that

I can't see anything wrong with me, – Mum is the only one in the house suggesting it, . . . it makes me feel bad towards Mum, I wonder what she's doing this for.

In another case a psychologist recommended a child's placement in a residential school on the grounds that the child showed signs of having 'psychiatric disorder'. However, in commenting on his recommendation to a researcher he stated, in his opinion, that the disorder was not itself the reason for the placement as appropriate forms of therapy could easily be delivered. The real problem that made a residential school placement necessary was 'the disordered family environment'. No mention was made of this in the psychologist's advice to the LEA because the psychologist believed that if the parents felt they were being blamed for their child's difficulties their already strong resistance to residential schooling would be further reinforced. By identifying the problem entirely in terms of a psychiatric disorder, the psychologist argued that the parents would be more likely to accept the recommended placement, which they could agree to without having to accept any blame.

Teachers differ as to whether they prefer to see children as 'emotionally disturbed' or as 'behaviourally disordered'. Kugelmass (1987), who studied an urban North American school with a programme for severely emotionally disturbed children, found that the teachers preferred to think of the children as having behaviour disorders, as they could observe behaviour but could only hypothesise about emotional difficulties. However, she also noted that subjective judgements were used to decide which behaviour was defined as 'disordered'. In our study, teachers generally preferred to understand children's behaviour in terms of emotional difficulties either within the child or within the family. A common characteristic of teacher accounts was their reference to circumstances over which they had no control and for which they felt they could not be held responsible.

Race and gender

Those attempting to understand the assessment process for children thought to 'have EBD' have consistently noted that certain groups of pupils are more likely to be labelled as disruptive, maladjusted, difficult or emotionally and behaviourally disturbed. The pupils are clearly defined in socio-economic, ethnic and gender terms. An historical survey of those more likely to be defined as disruptive shows clearly that it has always been poor and working-class male pupils who were considered to have non-conformist behaviour, and since the arrival of Afro-Caribbean pupils in the 1960s, black working-class boys have also been regarded as problematic in schools and more likely to be candidates for special education. Initially Afro-Caribbean pupils were over-referred for ESN-M schooling. They were over-represented in such schools by a factor of four (Tomlinson, 1982).

Following well-publicised objections from black parents, referrals for this type of special education dropped, but referrals of black pupils as maladjusted and as EBD increased and they were more likely than other pupils to be suspended or excluded from schools on behavioural grounds. A study commissioned for the Commission for Racial Equality reported that black pupils were five times more likely to be placed in units for disruptive pupils in Birmingham (CRE, 1985). Wright (1986) reported that black pupils were four times more likely than white pupils to be suspended in the two schools she studied, and in 1989 Nottingham Education Committee carried out an inquiry into their policies on exclusion and found that black boys were five times more likely than other groups to be excluded from Nottingham Secondary Schools (NCC, 1990). The Nottingham survey also indicated that over 80 per cent of excluded pupils lived in socially deprived areas. Other councils who have examined the results of their exclusion policies have reported a similar situation. In Wolverhampton, for example, Afro-Caribbean boys make up 6 per cent of the secondary school population but 12 per cent of exclusions. Researchers have found that black boys have been consistently regarded by teachers as more likely to present behaviour problems than other pupils. Bagley (1982) used data from the National Child Development study in which teachers had described their Afro-Caribbean pupils as 'delinquent, rebellious and aggressive', and Tomlinson (1981a) found that teachers were more likely to regard black boys as aggressive. She noted (p. 305) that

> the stereotyped beliefs which professional people hold about West Indian children's ability, behaviour and attitudes to education, together with an acceptance that these are somehow 'natural racial attitudes', have made it more likely that the children meet the referral criteria for special education.

The over-referral of white working-class boys and the small numbers of white and Asian girls referred as behaviour problems has also been well documented (Ling and Davis, 1984; DES, 1989b), and in a recent study Cooper *et al.* (1991) sampled 355 'EBD' schools and behavioural units and found black boys again over-represented, with black girls also being over-represented in this type of education.

In attempting to understand why teachers find the behaviour of particular social, ethnic and gender groups threatening or disturbing in class, and more willing to assign them the social identity of EBD, it becomes very difficult to sustain a medical or a psychological model for understanding the 'causes' of such behaviour. The situation can only be interpreted in terms of interpersonal interactions and of school participation in the social construction of deviant behaviour, and must take into account teachers' beliefs and perceptions of different racial, ethnic, gender and socio-economic groups. Hargreaves and his colleagues (1975) discussed the way in which teachers develop typologies of students, and how some pupils are stereotyped as deviant or potentially deviant at an early age. The labelling is often done on the basis of teacher assumptions and beliefs rather than actual behaviour. Pupils from families about whom teachers have positive assumptions – for example, white middle-class girls – are considered to be 'out of character' if they misbehave, whereas black working-class boys are held to be demonstrating some underlying natural 'racial' characteristics. In the longer term teachers' perceptions of pupils can create a self-fulfilling prophecy and the pupils can react by adopting the deviant identity assigned to them.

Pupil views

How pupils undergoing assessment as potentially EBD perceived the process and were involved in the creation of their new social identity was a major concern in the study reported in this book. The data provide an objective test of the view expressed by the DES (1989a) that 'the feelings and perceptions of the child should be taken into account during the assessment procedures'. It also raises questions as to how far it is possible for children to participate in a process which designates them as 'bad' or 'naughty' – in essence accepting and perpetuating the idea that they are socially disorganising for others, and morally worthless themselves, and that they undermine an accepted social order. Bogdan and Kugelmass (1984) have noted that 'society has traditionally been structured to bring shame to those with alleged disabilities' (p. 189). How are we to understand the views of children invited to participate in constructing an identity for themselves which is not only shameful, but also intrinsically 'bad'? Although most of the participants in the assessment process – especially the parents and children – are unaware of the history of the EBD category and its unpleasant and stigmatic connotations, it is a serious question as to whether it is possible for children to have positive feelings about the creation of such a negative and 'spoiled' identity for themselves.

There has been very little discussion and virtually no research into how children perceive the acquisition of their special education labels and how far the public identity imposed on them by the assessment process is congruent with their own private self-identity. It is likely, however, that although social psychologists accept that individuals have multiple social identities, that acquired via a special, particularly an EBD, label is likely to be one of the most deeply felt and all-encompassing identities.

Stigmatisation, labelling and differential treatment are, of course, felt by pupils all through the 'normal' school system. Hargreaves (1982) has written strongly about the social and personal implications for pupils of labelling in comprehensive schools. 'Ability labels are not seen by pupils as mere descriptions of part of their total set of attributes as human beings: they are seen rather as generalised judgements, (p. 62). Pupils labelled as low-ability or academic rejects – the vast majority being from working-class homes – have their dignity damaged, and 'when dignity is damaged, one's deepest experience is of being inferior, unable and powerless'' (p. 17).

If this is true of those deemed to be 'less able', how much more true must it be for pupils who are asked to accept that they are disturbed and disruptive, and what kind of dignity and positive feelings can these children retain?

It must be asked why, despite a rhetoric post-1981 of consultation with parents and pupils, parents still feel pressured by 'experts', pupils are generally not consulted, and, on the whole, parents and children come to accept negative labels and identities. Part of the answer to this question lies in the nature of professionalism (which will be further discussed in Chapter 8) by which the claims that professionals are always acting 'in the child's best interests' and that they are applying their expert knowledge, are taken very seriously by both parents and pupils. The children in our study had certainly internalised the idea that professionals 'know best' and must ultimately be deferred to. Most children had also internalised the idea that they had a personal deficit causing problems for others and that the professionals would 'find out what was wrong with me'.

Where a child did hazard a guess as to 'what was wrong', a specific label or disability, which was not as pejorative as the EBD label, was usually fixed on. Thus several children thought they might be 'dyslexic', a term currently enjoying media publicity, and ascribed their problems to 'dyslexia'. Their reactions were similar to those reported by Jenkins (1991) who asked mentally handicapped young people what the term meant. These young people responded with apparent incomprehension or fixed on a specific and visible issue such as 'wheelchair' or difficulty with speech and reading. The young people in our study were similar to those in Jenkins's study in that they were generally not fully aware of how they were perceived by professionals and the public, and did not realise the extent to which the label would affect their social and economic positions.

Conclusions

The social consequences of being assessed and placed in a special education category, particularly one with the historical stigmatic connotation of EBD, are long-term and potentially harmful to the individual. Despite the humanitarianism apparently contained in the notion of 'catering for special needs' or 'acting in the child's best interests', children receiving the label become marginalised members of the society. The stigmatic social identity becomes a means by which children can be segregated from their peer group, friends, home and local community, denied access to the educational experiences offered to 'normal' children and offered a curriculum which may subsequently deny them access to further education, training or most types of employment.

Those who actually benefit from the marginalisation of troublesome pupils are the school and teachers whose rigid institutional practices and curriculum (particularly the National Curriculum and its assessment practices) can continue unimpeded and unchanged. It is entirely understandable, given social and political expectations, that schools will control their pupils and enable as many of them as possible to gain qualifications at higher and higher levels, and that any child perceived to be a problem will be a candidate for removal.

There is also some evidence that, in the short term, some children do benefit from the changed social situation of segregated 'EBD' education. However, it is hypocritical to continue to pretend that the assessment and labelling of children as EBD is solely for their 'good', rather than the 'good' of the wider educational system and ultimately the wider society.

In the final chapters of this book we focus on problems inherent in *every* education system which aims to cater for pupils with a wide range of abilities, expectations, beliefs and behaviour. We have already shown that assessment is a social process with social consequences, which is true irrespective of any special education legislation. Is it not possible to envisage large groups – educational, leisure or industrial – in which members form no evaluative judgements about each other and in which social identities do not develop as a result of such judgements? The task of the school system is to ensure as far as possible that the evaluative judgements which teachers, inevitably, form about their pupils, do not launch pupils on a descending spiral of educational attainment and social behaviour. Unfortunately, this is precisely what sometimes appears to happen.

CHAPTER 8

Professional cultures and their consequences

Introduction

We have argued that social identities are inherent in any social grouping. An important aspect of this process is the 'culture' which develops within a group as a way of maintaining and developing solidarity among its members. The culture is embedded in a set of attitudes and behaviour which a group's members are expected to adopt. It can be seen in the groups of disaffected teenagers described by Willis (1977) or Corrigan (1979), who pride themselves on their rejection of their school's official rules and values. It can also be seen in a different form in other groups of pupils who encourage each other in their participation in curricular and extra-curricular activities. The same process is evident in groups of workers, whether manual, 'white collar' or professional.

A professional culture is integral to any professional grouping. How it develops depends on the demands made on its members, and on the stresses they experience. The culture that develops in a school in which teachers expect most pupils to progress to well-known universities differs from that in schools in which they expect most pupils to leave for unemployment or a temporary training scheme at 16. It is clear, though, that if an education system claims responsibility for *all* children, there are implications for the professional cultures that develop among teachers and other professionals. This is partly because 'special' pupils pose a threat as well as a challenge within a school. Their needs can be seen in different ways by different professions, and indeed by different members of the same profession. Conflict is inherent in decisions about special educational provision. In this chapter we explore some of the consequences for pupils and the implications for professional priorities and practice.

Professionals and their judgements are indispensable to the assessment process for special education, particularly when the assessment leads to Statementing. It is the professional status of the assessors which legitimates the complex procedures which have been developed to exclude or marginalise pupils from ordinary classrooms, or at least to make their presence contingent upon additional resources.

The major professional groups dealing with the assessment of children for special education during the twentieth century have been medical doctors, educational psychologists, and teachers, in both

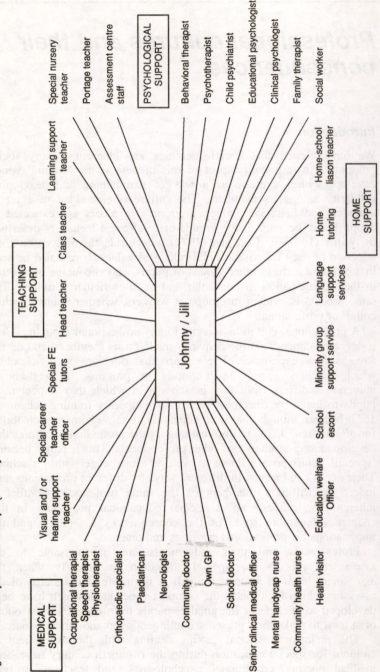

Figure 8.1 Possible professional help for Johnny / Jill

mainstream and special education – and their work has been embedded in a bureaucracy which includes administrators at local (LEA) levels and policy-makers at both local and central levels. As the century progressed more and more professionals, and 'semi-professionals', as Etzioni (1969) dubbed some of the newer professions, have come to claim expertise in dealing with children in need of, or thought to be in need of, some form of special education. Much of the now compulsory component on 'special educational needs' in all initial teacher training actually consists of informing teachers about the variety of other professionals whose help they can call upon if they cannot cope with troublesome pupils.

This chapter briefly notes the expansion of professional groups who deal with children thought to have 'special educational needs', the development and characteristics of professions, some 'models' of professionalism and the ambiguous position of professionals working within a system that lacks any clear policy framework either at central or local level. The chapter concludes that if professionals are to live up to ideals of service and social justice they may have to question their position as gatekeepers of resources on behalf of LEAs and schools.

The expansion of professionalism

Over the past 20 years more professionals have joined the older established professions in claiming a legitimate involvement in special education processes. They constitute what can be, for parents and children, a formidable proliferation of expertise. Figure 8.1 illustrates the variety of professional services which could, theoretically, be made available to deal with 'Johnny or Jill' should he or she require them. An expanded variety of medical, psychological, teaching support services and home support services is available to deal with special children from pre-school to further education and adult life. It is perhaps unsurprising that in 1990–91 approximately £1.5 billion was spent on provision for special needs pupils (AC–HMI, 1992).

Each professional group has its own 'culture of professionalism' (Larson 1977), which includes specialised training, its own esoteric language, and its own claims to expert practice. Each professional expects his or her judgement to be accepted and respected by the clients – children and parents – and by other professionals. An over-arching ideology, or generalised belief, that unites all the professionals, is that whatever they do they will be acting 'in the best interests of the child'. Since much of the study reported in this book has indicated that the assessment processes can give rise to conflicts of interest, that the 'smooth teamwork' envisaged by the Warnock Committee (DES, 1978) is difficult to achieve, and that it is questionable whether professional judgements are always made in the best interest of the child, it is important to include in our book some general considerations of professionals and their practices.

A major issue in the study of professionalism concerns definitions of the term 'professional'. Given that there has been a proliferation of groups claiming professional skills, ideals and status, but employed by large organisations or state bureaucracies, it is a pertinent question to ask: What exactly is a professional? The classic nineteenth-century self-employed professional, typified by medicine or the law, is not an appropriate way of understanding the modern professional. There are a large number of new professions who share some, if not most, of the characteristics of other professions, but all professions now depend to a large extent on employment by the state. Speech therapists and health workers, for example, could sell their skills privately, yet claim to serve the public, just as doctors or lawyers can do, but there is still debate as to how far they are simply an occupational category rather than a profession. Larson (1977) developed the notion of 'organisational professional' to describe the way in which groups as varied as hospital administrators, college presidents, librarians and social workers, could all claim professional characteristics while working within state bureaucracies. This, however, leads to a second important issue which concerns the relationship between professionals and bureaucracies. How are professionals used by government departments and local authorities?

The development and characteristics of professions

One of the major aspects of the occupational structure of modern societies is the growth of professionals and professionalisation. The American sociologists Faunce and Clellan noted in 1967 that this growth involved:

- more job specialisation with an increasing proportion of professionals and technicians in the labour force
- a status system in which being a professional and gaining professional recognition is important
- a power structure in which professionals have increasing influence
- a class structure in which class distinctions are increasingly based on access to education and higher level qualifications.

Understanding the expansion and development of different professional groups does mean accepting that professions, particularly the older, more established ones, do have a good deal of power over their clients and that their judgements will affect the future lives of people who are subordinate to these judgements. It also means understanding that the class and status positions of professions are important. Larson pointed out that professions are not joint occupational categories, 'whatever they are, professions are situated in the middle and upper middle levels of the stratification system' (Larson, 1977, p. xvi) and individual professional status is undeniably a middle-class attribute. Since, by definition, once people acquire the education and training required to join a profession they leave the working class, a relative superiority over and distant from the working (and non-working) class is one of the major characteristics of all professions. In special education in all the Western industrial societies, the majority of the clients dealt with by the various professionals are in the lower socio-economic groups; and in the USA, Europe and Australia, where large numbers of ethnic minority pupils are processed into special education, the professional groups are not only middle class but are also predominantly white.

The parents of children being assessed for and placed in special education are likely to have had little education, to defer to the knowledge and expertise of professionals, and to acknowledge the professionals' higher social status. This creates an immediate difficulty when professionals are exhorted to 'treat parents as equals' and involve them in decision-making. It is also likely that parents from working-class backgrounds cannot negotiate easily with professionals as they do not have available what Fulcher (1989) has called a 'discourse of democratisation' to assert their views and rights. It was noticeable, in the study reported in our book, that parents who did wish to challenge professional views, had to 'feel their way around' situations with which they were unfamiliar, and try out strategies to challenge professional judgements. Because they had no experience of a professional culture they were at a disadvantage in ways which even the professionals themselves did not fully understand.

Professions then, are generally higher status, middle-class occupations granted special powers and prestige, and although the characteristics of professional groups vary, there is substantial agreement about what makes a profession. These characteristics include having expert esoteric knowledge and techniques, acquired through a specialised training, an esoteric language (or jargon), a claim to autonomy and the right to control the work done, an ethical code and a service ideal. Thus, professionals claim expert knowledge and profess to know better than others what is wrong with their clients. Armed with their expert knowledge, professionals ask to be trusted and do not expect their clients to question their judgements. Professionals not only claim to know better, but also are allowed to define the standards by which their superior competence is judged. Thus, educational psychologists have, during the twentieth century, claimed an expertise in IQ testing and have defined their competencies in knowing better than others, how to measure levels of 'intelligence'. Professionals who deal with 'dyslexic' children are currently laying claims to new competencies in defining and treating dyslexia (Klein, 1992).

Professional associations insist on a lengthy training through which their particular body of knowledge and techniques are communicated, and the training is usually under the control of professional bodies. Debates over the professionalism of teachers centre round the absence of control over training by a professional teaching association, the state increasingly defining teachers' roles and duties in Britain. However, teachers, in common with other professionals, acquire and use a specialist vocabulary and language which sets them apart from the uninitiated. The creation of a 'professional mystique' is important as professional powers and privileges depend on an ability to create an aura of mystery around the work, and language plays an important role in the creation of the mystique. Habermas (1974) has examined in some detail the way those with authority legitimate their actions and the way they use language to dominate and control. In special education, the use of a 'treatment language', carried over from medical discourse, is a powerful tool for professionals. Habermas also pointed out that the use of professional language can be a cover to prevent an open discussion of 'what is really going on'. In special education practices, 'what is going on' is frequently an attempt by professionals to persuade clients to accept certain judgements without recourse to actual coercion. Special education is an area to which clients seldom come voluntarily, and enforceable procedures, legal sanctions which can force parents to accept special education for their children, have been built into Education Acts in 1914, 1921, 1944, 1981 and 1988. The sanction of enforceable procedures has always conflicted with professional claims that assessments or practices are motivated solely by humanitarian concerns. Professionals seldom mention to parents that coercion can be used if persuasion, fortified by superior knowledge and treatment language, fails to convince.

Despite the possibilities of coercion, professionals working in special education share with all other professionals the characteristics of the 'service ideal'. Professionals claim a degree of altruism and a disinterestedness from wider social, political and economic considerations. They consider that they are working solely in the interests of the client. The service ideal is based on both a professional code of ethics and also the idea of ethical neutrality – professionals do not condemn or judge out of prejudice – they make judgements based on their expertise, 'doing their best' for the client. We have already recorded that the professionals to whom we talked in our study professed this service ideal; they claimed that their overriding concern was 'to act in the interests of the children and involve parents at the centre of decision-making' (Armstrong and Galloway, 1992a).

Models of professionalism

It is important to consider what sort of models, or exemplary understandings of the framework in which they work, professionals involved in special education actually have in mind, and how the various professional groups perceive and react to each other.

The archetypical nineteenth century professional groups – notably medicine and the law – were, in modern terms, self-employed capitalists who nevertheless presented an anti-market image and distanced themselves from the developing bureaucratic practices of the state. Indeed, professionals regarded themselves, and some still do, as the antithesis of the bureaucratic modes of 'people-processing' which have little regard for individual feelings or interests. However, professionals involved in special education have increasingly been drawn into the service of local and central bureaucracies whose concerns are with the wider education system and with wider social, political and economic considerations.

There is a long history of interprofessional rivalry for domination of the assessment procedures (Pritchard, 1963; Tomlinson, 1982) but by 1944 medical influence was paramount. Psychologists were claiming parity with doctors, teacher influence was minimised but educational administrators had extended their influence through the control of resources. By the 1980s medical influence on assessment procedures had declined, psychological influences had extended and teacher involvement was again important. The role of the LEA administrator, following changes in the funding of education after the 1988 Act, had become crucial, although the question of whose professional judgements are most important is still a contested professional issue.

The expense of employing a variety of professionals to test, observe and interview children and parents, write Statements and hold meetings and case conferences, has increased considerably over the years, although LEAs have been reluctant to cost this, since the assessment process provides the ammunition which rationalises the giving or withholding of other resources. Assessment decisions by professionals are increasingly embedded in the financial needs of local authority bureaucracies (AC–HMI, 1992).

The over-arching model of professional involvement in special education was neatly captured by Kirp in 1983, who, after comparing the situation in the USA and the UK, wrote that:

the model of professionalism involved in the UK is essentially a humanitarian welfare model which contemplates professionals and administrators working on behalf of an ever-expanding clientele towards an agreed common goal . . . in moulding special education policy in Britain, professionalism, entwined with the bureaucratic structure, has enjoyed near-absolute pre-eminence as a policy frame. (Kirp, 1983, p. 83)

This model, as Kirp pointed out, takes no account of any issues of civil rights, or parental rights backed by the law. Kirp noted that the Warnock Committee, who 'visited the USA in the 1970s' came away horrified at the reliance on administrative hearings and litigation, ' . . . in the framework of the Warnock Report, rights would war with the idea of efficient service provided by professionals acting to the best of their abilities' (Kirp, 1983, p. 94). Indeed, Mary Warnock herself declared in an interview with Kirp that 'there is something deeply unattractive about the spectacle of someone demanding his own rights' (p. 95).

A 'rights' framework for special education, which is overtly political, emerged in the USA following the Civil Rights Act and has been slowly emerging as a possible alternative framework to 'humanitarian bureaucracy' in Western Europe and Australia. As Fulcher has noted, 'the rights discourse is seen as the most progressive and obvious strategy for those excluded from full citizenship in modern welfare states' (Fulcher, 1989, p. 31). The entire manner in which professionalism operates in special education has been subjected to a stringent critique by Fulcher. The incorporation of professionals into the bureaucratic practice of control and regulation of large groups of people via welfare state services have, in her view, assisted in the process of marginalising the disabled and the special, and have helped to disempower clients and prevent democratic educational practices which would make assessment for exclusion unnecessary (Fulcher, 1989, pp. 226–32).

There is some evidence that alternative frameworks within which assessment decisions can be made are gradually emerging in Britain, as parents increasingly turn to litigation to clarify the 'right' to particular kinds of provision or levels of resources for their Statemented children. Professionals, too, may be thinking of themselves in terms of advocates for rights as well as humanitarian bureaucrats. Armstrong and Galloway (1992a) reviewed models of professional relationships relating both to the study reported in this book and to other studies, and noted that psychologists, psychiatrists and social workers, while still subscribing to doctor–patient models of treatment, and to resource-management models, were also seeing themselves as advocates, consultants and protectors of clients' rights.

Professional conflicts

A major area of conflict for professionals continues to be with parents. On face value the 1981 Act formalises a cooperative relationship with parents, parents being ostensibly drawn into the assessment process with legal rights and responsibilities. In practice, as Armstrong and Galloway (1992b) have noted, 'the bureaucratisation of the professional–parent relationship and of the assessment process may lead to a situation in which the primary function of parental involvement is to legitimatise professional decisions' (p. 193). In our study many parents felt that their own contribution to assessment was only listened to when they were confirming professional views or decisions and professionals continued to divert or persuade parents towards a seeming consensus, in which parents often felt they had no choice but to agree. The unique power position, the position of professionals as gatekeepers of crucial information, and the almost foregone conclusion that a child's 'needs' will be subordinate to the perceived 'needs' of schools and teachers, negated the notion of parents as equal partners in the assessment process. Ultimately professionals know that in any conflict of interest, they have the sanction of coercion against uncooperative parents.

The ambiguous position of 'organisational professionals' who are in effect 'paid servants of the state' and who carry out their work within the bureaucratic structures of local government, is a potential source of conflict between professionals and administrators and between professionals and their clients. Psychologists are in a particularly ambiguous situation. In Chapter 6 we documented the conflicting demands made upon one psychologist in his assessment of 'Ben' (Armstrong and Galloway 1992a). In this particular case the LEA considered the psychologist to be a consultant who would provide advice that could be used for resource decisions; the child's parents regarded him as an LEA officer working on behalf of the LEA rather than their child; and the teachers regarded him as the professional who would work in their interests to secure extra resources for the school. The Audit Commission, in a recent report on provision made by LEAs for pupils with special educational needs, noted that while

the educational psychology (sic) service has a pivotal role in deciding with schools and parents whether it is appropriate formally to assess a child, in some LEAs, psychologists have not taken this role either through fear of conflict with the schools, or because the LEA has had no policy on which to base their position (AC–HMI, 1992).

LEA policy – particularly after 1988 when local management of schools was introduced – has been totally finance driven as regards assessment for special needs and LEAs have been unable to produce coherent policies. The 1981 Act and the Statementing process which required professionals, on behalf of LEAs, to specify provision, was theoretically a blank cheque whereby parents could demand, or professionals recommend, levels of provision which the LEA could not afford. LEAs have therefore chosen to use psychologists as gatekeepers of resources, attempting to ensure that the wording on Statements concerning provision was vague enough to keep costs down, and to delay the completion of Statementing. There is evidence that psychologists who refuse to comply with LEA directives on recommendation for provision can find their jobs in jeopardy (Pyke, 1990). Professionals working within bureaucracies are certainly subject to many more conflicts and ambiguities than the old-style self-employed professional.

The service ideal revisited

The 1981 Education Act ostensibly ushered in an era of improved practice in dealing with children who, pre-1981, were ascertained as belonging to a particular category of handicap, and the larger number who were remedial or disruptive in school. The egalitarian notion of integration was intended to help retain as many children as possible in mainstream education, with appropriate support. However, the failure of central government to develop national policy, and the finance-driven and bureaucratic procedures of local education authorities who lacked a definition of 'special educational needs' and were unable to establish when Statements of special education were actually required, has led to the use of professionals involved in assessment as gatekeepers of local authority resources and as legitimators for the removal of 'difficult' children from mainstream education. Educational psychologists, in particular, have been expected to define provision in terms of available resources rather than the needs of children. Throughout the 1980s there has been an erosion of the 'service ideal' and an expansion of what could be considered an 'unprofessional' deference to central and local bureaucracy.

Professional groups involved in special education may well consider that it is time to take positive steps to assert those aspects of their professional cultures which really do benefit clients and distance themselves from becoming simply 'organisational professionals'. Some action which all professionals could unite in supporting are:

- a limitation on esoteric and mystifying language
- a genuine effort to inform parents and children about all aspects of referral, assessment and subsequent practice in special education and to regard parents as 'equal partners' rather than as clients to be persuaded
- a real consideration of the human and civil rights issues which would, in Britain, lead to a campaign to end enforceable procedures and the legal sanctions which currently are available to 'force' parents to accept special education for their children
- the use of professional skills and judgements to ensure that all children really do have access to a wide range of educational opportunities rather than the use of those skills as legitimators for segregation and exclusion.

The social welfare model of professionalism which assumes 'knowing what is best for the client' should now give way to a reassertion of the service ideal. A true professional commitment to this ideal should accept that parents and children – if properly enlightened – do have an informed view of their own interests and that professionals should work *with* their clients rather than against their interests as agents of bureaucracy. It will, for example, only be possible to offer all parents a real choice of schools for their children when enforceable procedures have been ended and an accurate assessment of parental support for schools and other provision separate from the mainstream is known.

If all professionals involved in special education demanded central and national policies for unified professional support for all kinds of children who have disabilities or attend schools which impede their learning, changes would occur. The increasing bureaucratisation of all educational practices:

stunts the growth of reflexive thought in society *and* in the professions which not only undercuts the ability of the public to govern itself democratically but further diminishes the capacity of professions to see themselves and their practices critically (Skrtic, 1991, p. 231)

A challenge to professionals may be to create a democratic professionalism to be set against an undemocratic bureaucracy.

Conclusions

This chapter has described the expanded 'organisational professionalism' which now characterises special education in Britain, and the way in which aspects of professional culture, notably the service ideal, has been subordinated to the requirements of bureaucracy, notably the financial needs of LEAs and the needs of schools to have troublesome children removed. The model of professionalism in special education practices in Britain continues to be that of an humanitarian welfare bureaucrat, heavily influenced by medical practices and a treatment language. A variety of new conflicts has been generated by the increased subordination of professionals to the state, including (a) a fragmented professionalism which encourages a division of responsibility for children rather than a professional care for the whole child, and (b) conflict with parents who still feel subordinate to professionals, are insufficiently consulted and informed, and have a role that is limited to acquiescence to decisions that have already been made. The whole coercive framework of special education continues to make nonsense of a rhetoric of parental involvement, partnership or choice. Educational psychologists, in particular, experience conflicts as they are expected to act as gatekeepers of local authority resources and are liable to be used as scapegoats for the lack of coherent policies on provision for special educational needs.

We conclude that social justice and democracy might be served if all professionals involved in special education based their actions on civil rights and a service ideal and, in particular, made efforts to end the use of legal coercive sanctions to enforce provision outside the mainstream education system.

C H A P T E R   9

Multidisciplinary assessment: is it justified?

Introduction

Legislation, the rhetoric of countless government reports and common sense dictate that members of different professions should pool their knowledge and expertise in reaching an understanding of children's needs and how they should be met. Special educational needs may be associated with social and medical problems as well as with cognitive ability and behaviour. Assessment by a multidisciplinary team would appear to be the *sine qua non* for good practice. Yet it remains an ideal rather than a reality.

We argued in Chapter 8 that developing a professional culture is both inevitable and necessary if a profession is to claim expertise and social status. One of the consequences of professional cultures is that they lead to rivalry between professions. When the outcome of an assessment is constrained by the availability of resources, the scope for interdisciplinary collaboration is further reduced, leading to new conflicts over professional identity.

In this chapter we shall argue that the origins of multidisciplinary assessment lie in interdisciplinary conflict. The ideal of the multidisciplinary assessment is derived from a genuine concern that the needs of the 'whole child' should be looked at. In practice, however, procedures may focus principally upon negotiations over areas of professional responsibility in the context of the management of resources. Often these negotiations are not contentious insofar as they take place against a background of previous negotiations that have established the 'rules of engagement'. Exceptions occur, however, where the child is perceived to have different, possibly conflicting, needs and these needs are identified as lying principally within the domain of more than one professional group.

Multidisciplinary assessment: Its origins in conflict

There is a long history of interprofessional rivalry for control of the special education assessment procedures (Pritchard, 1963; Tomlinson, 1982). The outcome of this rivalry between different professionals within the assessment 'team' has largely reflected the power of those groups at different times rather than the need for a whole-child assessment. For example, while in the early 1890s the 'team' of professionals involved in the assessment of 'mentally defective' children included a doctor and the head teacher of the referring and the special school, teachers were gradually excluded from assessment decisions. In 1896 a government-appointed Department Committee on Defective and Epileptic Children recommended that the selection of children for a special school should be undertaken by a doctor. This early domination of thinking about special education by medical professionals established a discourse of 'needs' in terms of handicaps that continued well into the twentieth century.

The profession of educational psychology, which later was to play such a leading role in the decision-making process, was at that time in its infancy, and in particular the techniques of 'mental measurement' which were to become the basis of its later claim to specialised professional knowledge had not yet been developed. However, by the early 1920s the dominance of the medical profession in this area began to be challenged by the emerging profession of educational psychology based on the revolutionary work of Cyril Burt. By 1944, although medical influences remained paramount, the challenge from educational psychology was becoming increasingly vocal as psychologists claimed parity with doctors. Educational administrators had also extended their role through the control they were able to exercise over the allocation of resources. By contrast, teacher influence during this period was minimised.

Under the 1944 Education Act medical officers were the only professionals to have statutory powers to decide that a child was suffering from 'a disability of body or mind'. However, Circular 2/75 (DES, 1975) clearly represented an attempt to substitute an educational model of assessment for the medical model that had previously been dominant, effectively changing the balance of power between doctors and psychologists within these procedures. Where parents objected to a professional recommendation for special school placement the statutory power to certify a child's category of handicap and prescribe special education remained with doctors. In practice this was a power that had seldom been exercised and Circular 2/75 embodied the DES view of good practice in assuming a consensus would be reached between professionals (Galloway and Goodwin, 1987). More importantly, Circular 2/75 recommended the introduction of a new assessment form summarising the educational, medical and psychological reports. This summary form was to be prepared for the LEA by an experienced psychologist or adviser on special education. This recommendation created a struggle for control between educational psychologists and LEA advisers. The 1981 Education Act created the possibility of by-passing both these professional groups by giving responsibility for decisions on resources and where they should be provided to the chief education officer. In practice this usually meant a member of the LEA's administrative staff, though in one of the LEAs which took part in the research described in this book the educational psychologists retained responsibility.

In practice, Circular 2/75 frequently fuelled interprofessional rivalries rather than clarifying the procedures to be adopted within the assessment. The considerable autonomy of education authorities, as well as the relative autonomy of education and health authorities within the local authority structure, meant that power struggles between the rival professions continued unabated. The antagonisms between head teachers, doctors, psychologists and other personnel as they wrestled for influence within the assessment procedures has been documented by Tomlinson (1981a) in her study of the decision-making process in special education. Thus a special school head thought 'some psychologists are way out and autocratic' (p. 232), a doctor believed 'psychologists are taking over from us' (p. 92) and a psychologist found 'doctors are sometimes annoyingly irrelevant' (p. 162). Classroom teachers felt de-skilled and ignorant in any subsequent decision-making and action. Elsewhere Tomlinson (1981b) has argued that interprofessional rivalries and conflicts are themselves the source of particular constructions of children's needs. The label attached to a child by the assessment, she argues, serves to legitimate the role of the particular professional whose professional interests are represented by the label. Thus conflict between professionals focuses upon 'the status of professional judgements and the power implicit in these judgements which legitimizes the complex procedures which make the categorisation an objective reality' (p.11).

Yet, in spite of the reality of interprofessional rivalry, the rhetoric remained that of cooperation. The Plowden Report (CACE, 1967), for example, regarded partnership between professionals as central in alleviating the consequences of social disadvantage. It was an ethic rooted in a consensus model of social reform in which cooperation between professionals was derived from a conception of their common interests in maximising client opportunities. As the Court Report (DHSS, 1976) later maintained

... to disentangle the strands [that make up children's needs] is beyond any single expertise. Medical, Social and Psychological advice have therefore to be available if the child is to receive the best education that can be offered. (para 10:39)

Multidisciplinary assessment under the 1981 and 1993 Acts

The 1981 Education Act, heavily influenced by the Warnock Report (DES, 1978), took on board many of its recommendations, including its support for multidisciplinary assessment procedures. Schedule 1,1(2) of the 1981 Education Act requires local education authorities, once they have initiated the formal assessment of a child's special educational needs, to 'seek medical, psychological and educational advice and such other advice as may be prescribed'. The 1993 Act has a similar requirement.

The commitment here to the principle of multidisciplinary assessment is clear. Once a child has been referred for assessment the LEA is to have at its disposal the services of a wide range of professional advisers who will, from their own specialised perspectives, contribute to building up a full picture of the child's needs. Equipped with a broad range of information about a child's needs the LEA will be in a much better position to make decisions about the most effective use of its resources in meeting the special educational needs that have been identified. What this means for the organisation of the assessment team, however, is left vague.

In its advice to LEAs on the implementation of the 1981 Act, the DES (1989) offered the following guidance:

By bringing together the skills, perceptions and insights of professionals in different disciplines, as well as those of the parents, it should be possible to arrive at a more complete understanding of a child's special educational needs. Effective multi-professional work requires co-operation, collaboration and mental support on the part of all contributors and should seek to reach agreement with them on their several roles and functions. It follows that the advice given by each one should reflect his or her concerns, leaving others to concentrate upon their particular area of expertise. (para. 51)

This advice closely follows the philosophy of the Warnock Report but it also suggests a rather oversimplified and naive view of interprofessional relationships.

By rejecting a medical model of children's special needs in favour of an educational model, the Warnock Report laid the foundations for a multidisciplinary approach to assessment which recognised the importance of assessing the whole child. The multidisciplinary team envisaged by the Warnock Committee was to include not only a range of professionals – teachers, psychologists, doctors, etc. – but also the child's parents, who were seen as contributing their own 'expert' knowledge of the child to the assessment. The re-conceptualisation of 'needs' advocated by the Warnock Report, together with the recommendations made for identifying them, had two major implications for the future role of special education.

First, it greatly increased the number of children who might potentially be identified as having special educational needs and therefore for whom a greater allocation of resources would be necessary. By abandoning the former categories the criteria for identifying special educational needs recommended by the Warnock Report were as open-ended as they were arbitrary. In effect they were to be a matter for negotiation between those involved in the assessment with the consequence that the professional assessment of children's needs could no longer be adequately understood solely in terms of the application of specialised systems of knowledge. This was to have considerable implications for the role of professionals carrying out assessments.

Second, Warnock's recommendation that special educational needs be de-medicalised and replaced with procedures for assessing educational needs not only created conditions in which the power of medical professionals, compared with that of teachers and psychologists, would be weakened but it also led to far greater emphasis being placed upon negotiations between professionals in the assessment procedures. Whatever the interests of the child, the interests of professionals would inevitably become tied to their ability to negotiate definitions of children's needs in terms of their own professional models. The criteria to be used to identify the child's needs would vary in each case depending upon the outcome of negotiations between the participants involved. These negotiations would not only lay the basis for interventions with the child but their outcome would also legitimate the dominant professional perspective underlying the consensus reached between the different professionals involved in the assessment. Recognition of this can be seen in the guarded response of the Association of Educational Psychologists to the Warnock Report. In spite of the recommendation contained in the Warnock Report that educational psychologists should play a key role in the assessment process and that their numbers should be doubled, the association expressed reservations about the suggestion that the multidisciplinary team *could* be coordinated by an LEA adviser as an alternative to the psychologist. A spokesperson for the association commented:

The association is likely to view with some scepticism the suggestion that a new breed of advisory teacher is necessary to facilitate communication between teachers and psychologists. (Education, 2 June 1978, p. 490)

Although this specific proposal was not in the event incorporated into the 1981 legislation, the response of the Association of Educational Psychologists does illustrate their concern, not only that they should have a clinical role in the assessment but that they should also be able to exercise power as decision-makers within that process. In this sense, whatever the intentions of the Warnock Committee in recommending multidisciplinary assessments, in practice, while the criteria used to identify children's needs were to be 'arbitrarily' decided, the multidisciplinary process would become a forum for negotiating areas of professional responsibility and control. The ideal of a multidisciplinary assessment of the whole child assumes, perhaps naively, that 'needs' are *identified* while ignoring the extent to which needs are *constructed* by the perspectives from which different professionals operate when carrying out their assessment. The significance of this interrelationship between professional perspectives, negotiation and decision-making is something that is entirely overlooked in the model of multidisciplinary assessment proposed by the Warnock Report and contained in the 1981 Education Act.

Implications for provision of resources

Reporting on the implementation of the 1981 Education Act, the House of Commons Education, Science and Arts Committee (HC, 1987) drew attention to a number of areas in which it was not working satisfactorily. One area was in the relationships between education, health and social services departments. Here the House of Commons Committee found that there were particular problems in resourcing Statements where recommendations were made for types of provision that were not directly available to the LEA. The provision of resources for speech therapy was found to be a particular source of difficulty but this reflected a more general failure of the agencies involved in special educational assessments to provide a coordinated service.

Probably the most comprehensive study of the implementation of the 1981 Education Act has been that by Goacher *et al.* (1988). They surveyed implementation of the 1981 Act in all English LEAs and in addition undertook a detailed review of policy and practice in five LEAs. They found that the quality of multidisciplinary involvement in the assessment procedures varied enormously but, overall, psychologists played the crucial role in formulating the views about children's needs subsequently set out in the Statements of special educational needs. Despite the emphasis in the 1981 Act on multidisciplinary involvement and cooperation, later backed up by advice from the DES on the implementation of the Act, Goacher *et al.* found little evidence to suggest that assessments involved anything more than 'collected' assessment, reports being compiled by individual professionals without consultation with colleagues in other agencies. 'Collective multiprofessional assessment', in which advice was formulated on the basis of on-going consultation and communication between professionals from different disciplines, was the exception:

Only in one of our detailed study areas was multi-service decision-making the norm ... case conferences ... (were) not a routine occurrence in any of the authorities. (Goacher *et al.*, 1988, p.111)

Moreover, in only 69 per cent of LEAs were steps taken to inform district health authorities of the outcome of assessments. Social services departments fared even worse, with only 50 per cent of LEAs passing on this information.

The absence of effective communications between different professional agencies may reflect, as Norwich (1990) has suggested, the lack of a shared understanding of ideas about special educational needs but, as he argues, such communication is itself dependent on the existence of effective cross-service interaction between education, health and social services. Goacher *et al.* (1988) also pointed to this lack of shared understandings but their findings indicated that the differences between agencies in their perceptions of who has specific responsibility were closely related to questions of how and by whom resources for children with special educational needs were to be financed.

Evidence from our own research suggests strongly that, where responsibility is clearly demarcated between agencies, the multidisciplinary component of an assessment is largely a bureaucratic exercise rather than one genuinely concerned with contributing an additional dimension to the procedures for identifying children's needs. For this reason it may be seen as largely irrelevant not only by education professionals but also by those professionals from outside the education service whose contributions are officially sought. The role of clinical medical officers in the assessment of emotional and behavioural difficulties, which we discuss in the following section, provides a good example of the bureaucratisation of the multidisciplinary assessment ideal. On the other hand, as we shall argue, where responsibility for meeting the child's needs, including both professional and financial responsibility, is unclear or contested the assessment procedures may then become a forum for negotiation between professionals about the authority and responsibilities of their respective agencies. While the outcome of these negotiations is usually concerned with the ownership and control of resources, the negotiations themselves are more likely to focus upon the professional role and authority of the different participants; in other words, upon ownership of the client. These negotiations illustrate what Fulcher (1989) has referred to as 'fragmented professionalism'. While explicit professional rivalry has been replaced by professional cooperation, negotiations between professionals over whether to accept or reject a client have become considerably more important – 'he's my child not yours' or conversely 'she's yours not ours'. A fragmentation of professional responsibilities clearly works against the professional service ideal and a responsibility for the 'whole child'.

The role of clinical medical officers

A medical examination forms a part of the statutory procedures of all assessments carried out under the provisions of the 1981 Education Act. The clinical medical officer (CMO), therefore, is a key member of the multidisciplinary team, at least in the sense that the assessment comprises a collected multidisciplinary assessment as described by Goacher *et al.* (1988). Certainly one might expect doctors to have an important role in assessments where educational needs are related to physical or sensory disabilities, although even here LEAs may be unwilling to accept advice that makes specific educational recommendations. In the assessment of physical and sensory disabilities medical advice may be seen as useful by LEAs insofar as, contrary to the spirit of the Warnock Report, it permits the application of criteria that can be used to plan the allocation of resources. The great majority of special education assessments, however, involve children whose difficulties fall into the non-normative categories of learning and behavioural difficulties, the definition of which presents particular problems. In our research, clinical medical officers relied mainly on checklists designed for the purpose within their district health authorities, together with a standard physical examination.

Interviews with CMOs, in our study of children assessed because of emotional and behavioural difficulties, revealed that they were generally unclear about their role in these assessments. CMOs frequently explained that they were reluctant to provide detailed accounts of children's needs for the LEA because they lacked confidence in their own professional expertise in a 'non-medical' area:

With behaviour cases I tend to leave it to the psychologist who is better qualified. I don't want to step on anyone's toes.

However, at least one doctor indicated that her reluctance had as much, if not more, to do with previous experiences of an LEA complaining about doctors exceeding their remit in making recommendations with resource implications for the LEA. In these circumstances the doctors to whom we spoke saw their contributions to the assessment of learning and behaviour difficulties purely in terms of screening for possible physical, neurological and psychiatric factors that had, until then, escaped recognition. In practice, even this role appeared to be constrained by a combination of factors including the CMO's lack of specialised knowledge and the absence, or limited availability, of specialist resources within the district health authority. These problems were summed up by a CMO who, in one case, wanted to recommend a referral to the local Child Guidance Clinic but nonetheless felt unable to make this recommendation in her report because:

The waiting list is over a year long, so from a medical point of view I would hesitate to refer because of lack of resources.

In another case, where a CMO firmly believed a child needed encouragement from the school if he was to overcome 'some real emotional difficulties', she remained silent about this in her discussions with LEA professionals and in her report to the LEA because of her conviction that the LEA would not tolerate that kind of judgement from someone who was not directly accountable for the resource implications of the recommendations being made.

As many as 8 of the 16 CMOs taking part in our study appeared to be unclear about their responsibilities under the 1981 Act and how these related to their general responsibilities within the district health authority. This could be seen, for instance, with regard to the procedures for seeking advice from, or making referrals to, psychiatric and paediatric specialists. One CMO in our study was concerned that a teenage girl whose special educational needs were being assessed was showing signs of a psychiatric disorder. Although the CMO believed that this disorder was a significant factor affecting the child's adjustment to school, she was nonetheless uncertain about what to do or say about it:

I would recommend that she is seen by a psychiatrist but I am not in a position to refer directly to a psychiatrist. I would suggest it to the educational psychologist. They should recommend it.

In the event she made no mention of her concerns either personally to the psychologist or in her advice to the LEA.

CMOs were more forthcoming about the personal values that guided their thinking about children with behaviour problems. For instance, one doctor made it clear when interviewed that

the professionals are standing up for the norms of society, the unwritten rules of the heart. These are akin to boundaries you do not cross, hitting, biting, spitting – things that save the culture. Having given them all the allowances I can, they didn't keep to the rules but behaviour modification will change that.

On the other hand, these opinions rarely came across in official reports:

I have to tell the truth but make sure that no one sues me.

In only three cases was the medical advice to the LEA accompanied by a specialist's report. In a further two cases reports had been requested from medical specialists by a CMO but had not been received before the Statementing procedures were concluded. The absence of these reports, although considered by the CMOs to have seriously impeded their ability to make proper judgements about the children's needs, did not appear to be matters of concern to either the non-medical professionals or to the LEAs. Indeed, there was some evidence to suggest that decisions were often made in principle and communicated informally to parents before *any* medical information was received. In part this occurred because education professionals felt that unreasonable delays by CMOs in making their reports added unnecessarily to the length of the Statementing procedures and added also to the anxieties and uncertainties suffered by children and their parents. However, in part, it also reflected the irritation of educational psychologists in particular over what was sometimes felt to be the unnecessary involvement of CMOs. In either event, these actions clearly reinforced the peripheral role of doctors in the assessment process. Perhaps not surprisingly, this caused particular annoyance to doctors. One CMO angrily observed:

The medical advice is lagging behind the action because the request for medical advice has come to me after the Statement has been enacted. The education authority has just gone ahead and bloody well done it.

By contrast teachers might involve doctors at a very early stage in order to pressurise their LEA into initiating a formal assessment. As one CMO commented:

Contact between professionals seems to depend upon the anxiety levels of the teachers. Sometimes they involve everybody immediately. If they've seen me it adds weight to their appeal for help.

The absence of genuine collective multidisciplinary procedures may be seen as reflecting the extent to which the assessment procedures are dominated by the administrative concerns and interests of the LEAs, and, in particular, by one professional group within those LEAs, namely psychologists. Studies since 1981, including our own research on the assessment of emotional and behavioural difficulties, have consistently drawn attention to the central role of psychologists in these procedures and to the power they have in determining the outcome of assessments. Taken in this context, the role of multidisciplinary assessment may be seen as having a quite different function to that of the collective assessment envisaged by the 1981 Act. This is suggested by Goacher *et al.* (1988) in respect of purposes of the assessment. These authors maintained that

... in addition to the overt functions of assessment ... there are other covert functions which relate more to the processes of negotiation and socialisation that occur as parents and professionals interact to achieve certain ends. These ends involve not only meeting the needs of individual children, but also the efficient management of resources and the reconciling of a variety of different interests. (p. 101)

The role of multidisciplinary assessment can be seen to operate in terms of very similar considerations, taking centre stage in those cases where it is necessary to reconcile the conflicting interests of different professional groups and administrative agencies to secure an efficient management of the resources available to the LEA. The most common context in which these negotiations take place is that between different professional groups within the education system, more especially between teachers and psychologists.

Negotiations between teachers and psychologists: studies in multidisciplinary assessment

The 1981 Education Act stipulates that where an LEA is considering issuing a Statement of special educational needs it must obtain educational advice, normally from teachers at the school the child is attending. The role of teachers in the assessment process, unlike that of medical professionals, is much more significant than consideration of their formal role in the procedures alone would suggest. The decision to refer a child for formal assessment is quite clearly a critical event having wide-ranging implications for that child's future. It also carries strong messages to other professionals who subsequently become involved in the assessment. Yet, teachers do not form a group whose interests are entirely homogeneous. The value attached to interprofessional cooperation by individual teachers may differ for ideological, professional and pragmatic reasons. There are occasions when teachers make a referral with the sole intention of seeking a second professional opinion on the child's needs. When Simon, one of the children in our own study, was referred to a psychologist by his school, his form teacher explained the reason for this referral as follows:

It was very important to get an official, an alternative view. We certainly found the psychologist useful in the past and we wanted to get her perspective.

By contrast the decision to refer a child may be taken in anticipation of a particular desired outcome, be it removal of the child from his or her school or the acquisition by the school of additional resources. This decision could reflect considerations other than immediate concerns about the school's ability to meet a child's needs at that time. This point can be illustrated by the comments of another of Simon's teachers, this time his head of year, whose responsibilities within the school forced him to view Simon's needs within the wider context of the LEA's policy and practice on allocating resources to schools.

If we are going to request Statementing to be commenced it is important to initiate the process before the end of a child's third year. After that, nobody really wants to know. Other children become priorities for resources.

In another case in the study, the desire of a classroom teacher to seek the advice and intervention of professionals from agencies outside the school arose from this teacher's lack of confidence in the head teacher's strategies for meeting the needs of a particular pupil. In this case the class teacher's referral of the child for formal assessment, although arising from a genuine concern for the child concerned, also reflected an attempt to negotiate a change in the school's policy on the identification of children with special needs. The involvement of outside agencies, particularly the schools' psychological service, was seen by the teacher as likely to empower her in these negotiations.

Where the decision to refer a child is taken in anticipation of its outcome, the assessment which follows may be seen as a bureaucratic process for effecting that outcome. Thus, in our study, multiprofessional assessments were often found to focus upon the negotiation of outcomes that were acceptable to teachers. Actions taken by the school prior to and during the assessment could be used quite explicitly to reinforce the negotiating position of teachers. There was evidence in nine cases of exclusions being used to force the pace of assessments. For example, one head teacher wrote to a child's parents notifying them of Michael's exclusion 'pending a psychologist's report'. In ten other cases exclusions were made in order to signal a school's unwillingness to readmit a child whose needs were being assessed.

While the 1981 Act suggests that multidisciplinary assessment should operate so that all aspects of the child's development and circumstances are examined, enabling a picture of the needs of the 'whole child' to be drawn, in practice informal negotiations between teachers and psychologists are perhaps the most significant multidisciplinary assessment events. The focus of these negotiations, however, is rarely upon a dispassionate assessment of the child's needs. The lack of any objective criteria for distinguishing between needs that are manageable with the resources normally available to a mainstream school and needs which require additional resources or specialist segregated provision means that the prime concern of teachers is often that of negotiating the dimensions of their responsibilities and professional role in individual cases.

Negotiating 'needs'

Bryan was 9 when his school referred him to the psychological service on the grounds of poor behaviour and associated learning difficulties. This was in fact the second time Bryan had been referred. Assessment procedures under the 1981 Act had been started at the school's request during the previous year but had not led to provision of a Statement because the psychologist thought he would make progress.

One reason I didn't wish to go ahead was that cognitively he could cope. Being in a new class might overcome the difficulties he had. I didn't feel his behaviour was quite in the same class as EBD kids.

Bryan's head teacher, on the other hand, maintained that Bryan

... can't do anything. ... If you are talking to him about something he'll go vacant.

In addition,

He's a biter. There have been a couple of times when he's kicked other children in the playground. Not just a kick. I've never seen children kicked as badly as that before. They were really bad incidents.

Thus, these comments revealed that there was a conflict between teachers and educational psychologist over what Bryan's needs were. Yet, they illustrate the attempts by each party to define the nature of need in Bryan's case and to form the expectations of the other in terms of their own perspectives. These perspectives became negotiable, however, when the action to be taken in response to Bryan's needs was discussed.

The head teacher argued that 'he should be in a special school really', and then somewhat ambiguously added, 'The problem is we can't get any special help for him until he's got a Statement.' The latter comment might have indicated a desire to transfer Bryan to a special school; on the other hand, it might have indicated a desire for help for the teachers themselves in meeting Bryan's needs. Whichever was the case, LEA policy in this borough did not require a Statement to be made in respect of a child before support could be made available within a school, either for learning difficulties or for behavioural problems.

The educational psychologist did not see Bryan's needs in terms of learning difficulties. He made this clear to the head teacher:

I think you should concentrate on the behaviour side of things. ... I don't think that we should be looking at an MLD school. ...

Now Bryan's needs were being redefined in terms of a broader conception of 'need' which included the teachers' perceptions of their own needs in meeting those presented by Bryan. This was acknowledged explicitly by the head teacher at the conclusion of the interview:

What is important is that the teachers get some support for Bryan in the classroom. We should have had that support before now. ... We can't be expected to teach him without extra help ... something will have to be done. The child has suffered and the teachers have suffered.

The resolution of the conflict over the meaning of 'needs' is brought about by a negotiated redefinition of the concept. In the first instance the educational psychologist was sceptical about the claims made by the head teacher concerning Bryan's learning difficulties. Moreover, she was concerned that a special school placement might not be the most appropriate course of action. On the other hand, the head teacher perceived the psychologist's previous decision not to proceed to formal Statementing as leaving the school without the resources or support to meet Bryan's needs in school. Thus, although a Statement was not necessary to obtain extra resources, the psychologist's decision not to recommend Statementing was seen by the head teacher as having undermined any claim the school might have had to LEA resources not Statement linked.

The complexity of this negotiation was acknowledged by the educational psychologist in the following comment to the researcher:

The head teacher ... wanted me to agree that Bryan is not appropriately placed in school. Afterwards she was quite happy with the prospect of getting extra resources for Bryan within the school. I think that's interesting. I wonder whether she might have wanted extra resources anyway at the beginning. She might have been laying it on a bit heavy about special schools for Bryan so as to force my hand to give her what she really wanted.

The negotiation over the meaning of 'needs' therefore was paralleled by a negotiation about resources. This leads us to a consideration of the interview's outcome and the negotiation of a consensus about this.

Negotiating outcomes

In Bryan's case it was agreed that for his needs to be met within the mainstream classroom it would be necessary to take account of and make provision for his teachers' perceptions of their own needs. Moreover, it was decided that extra resources, provided by outreach support, would be an appropriate way of meeting the needs that had been identified in the interview negotiation. The most important decision reached, however, was that Statementing procedures should be re-initiated.

On the face of it, the reason for this decision was not clear. A Statement of special educational needs was not required to obtain outreach support for Bryan either under the terms of the 1981 Act or to satisfy any conditions imposed within the borough in respect of the allocation of resources. Yet this outcome was central to the agreement that had been reached, and indeed was so much a part of the shared consensus about the outcome that neither party felt it necessary to explicitly define the purpose of the Statement in their discussions together.

At the initial stages of the interview the reason for proposing a Statement was presented more overtly by the head teacher. It was a necessary precondition for Bryan's placement in a special school. For the psychologist, on the other hand, it could have been a way of yielding to the pressure being exerted by the school without agreeing to any particular course of action. Embarking on a formal assessment of Bryan could be seen as a way of pacifying Bryan's teachers while influencing their perception of the issues:

In my psychological advice to the school I suppose I am trying to influence how the school perceives it.

By using the Statementing procedure as a way of influencing the thinking and action of others, the psychologist effectively redefined the purpose of the Statement in this particular case. A Statement is 'about extra resources within the education system' rather than about entry into a special school. The willingness of the psychologist to negotiate the purpose and role of the Statement was in part an acknowledgement of the teachers' power, a fact that he was well aware of:

It does make a difference how loud a teacher or head is prepared to shout. … In making a decision one of my criteria must be that those heads who shout the loudest get more.

It is also an acknowledgement of the teachers' needs:

As a psychologist I recognise that I am divorced from the classroom.

Developing from the interview is a shared conception of the purpose of Statementing that is linked to securing resources in response to both pupil and teacher needs within the school. The head teacher's view that 'the problem is we can't get special help for him until he's got a Statement' might be seen simply as a misconception of the 1981 Act. On the other hand, in terms of this particular interview, consensus over the appropriateness of a decision to proceed to formal Statementing arose from, and was integral to, the particular meaning that the educational psychologist and head teacher attributed to the role and purpose of the Statement. Thus, in this case, the provision of a Statement of special educational needs was perceived by both parties as formalising (and therefore safeguarding) the consensus negotiated within the interview and the expectations that each had of future events.

Multidisciplinary assessment as a forum for negotiating professional responsibilities

One agency that does not have a statutory role in the assessment of children with special educational needs is the local authority's social services department. They may, however, at the discretion of the LEA be asked to submit advice on a child where that child is known to them. In our study there were 11 such cases. The relationship between education authorities and social services departments may have ramifications for children with special educational needs that go well beyond the specific involvement of the latter in providing advice for individual Statements.

Where a social services department is providing support for a child within the family this involvement may make little difference to decisions arising from assessments of children's special educational needs. Information may be requested from the social services department and this may or may not be provided. From the standpoint of an evaluation of the effectiveness of multidisciplinary practice, these cases may raise questions about the flow of information between agencies, but the responsibilities of each agency for the child are likely to be clearly defined and demarcated. Where this is not the case, the absence or breakdown of communication between departments may result in delays in decisions being taken over the initiation of special needs assessments. A lack of communication between agencies could set up false expectations about the probable actions that each will take. From the perspective of educational professionals there may sometimes be a question mark over whether an educational assessment is appropriate. Where it is anticipated that other agencies will take certain actions, these may be seen as likely to pre-empt the need for further action by the education authority. Thus, in one case we followed, a psychologist complained bitterly that the involvement of social workers had led him to believe that the 'obvious social needs' of the child concerned would result in an application for a care order being made by social services. When this application did not materialise teachers at the child's school felt disappointed. In cases of this type social services departments were unwilling to adopt a high profile. In part, this reflected the demands placed on the resources available to social services departments; however, it often also reflected a commitment to the principle of maintaining parental responsibility for children's welfare other than in the most exceptional cases. Thus, an assessment of special educational needs leading to a residential school placement might, from the perspective of the social services department, be seen as preferable to a child being taken into care. Although there is a sense in which both outcomes would have the same effect, the former would not undermine the responsibilities of the parents towards their child.

The role of social services departments in relation to decision-making about children's special educational needs is at times ambiguous. For example, where social workers have a short-term role in providing care for a child – for instance, where a child has been placed in voluntary care by its parents – social workers may advise parents about the educational assessment but have not assumed full parental rights and so may not be directly involved in decision-making relating to educational needs and provision. However, there are times when LEA decisions about how educational needs are to be met can have a major influence on the type of family support which social services decides to offer. In one case, for example, a social worker wryly observed that:

Ideally I would have liked to keep Sean in [name of home town] but I wasn't aware of what [educational] provision was available.

The professional role adopted by social workers varied from case to case, but in those where they were providing family support they tended to adopt an advocacy role on behalf of the family. This could bring them into conflict with professionals from other agencies. Thus one social worker described special educational needs assessments as

all jargon and bureaucracy. Its exclusive of parents. There's a feeling that they're not going to be involved.

In consequence, this social worker saw his role as being 'to filter and translate' and became involved in the LEA's assessment (a) because he believed

there is a need to keep education and home linked

and (b) to provide support for a family in a situation characterised by 'verbal nodding and winking' as different professionals

try to persuade parents they are working in their best interests while covering up the lack of provision – making the best of a bad situation in the face of a lot of personal trauma.

Thus, social workers may understand their role in terms of empowering parents rather than in terms of facilitating the decision-making of other professionals. Those other professionals, however, could see this stance as a recipe for conflict:

it's as if they go into a case conference looking for a fight.

In other situations social workers came into conflict with educational professionals about the nature of the provision to be made available and by whom. Conflicts between the two departments over what, and whose, resources could or should be made available for a child very often reflected the considerable frustration felt by these professionals when the absence of adequate resources was perceived to interfere with their professional effectiveness. Where this occurred in our study the multidisciplinary component of the assessment took on a much higher profile as different agencies attempted to negotiate a consensus based upon their own individual assessments of the priorities in each case and the type of resources that could be made available to meet a wide range of identified needs.

The attempt by different agencies to use the multidisciplinary procedures to negotiate a consensus in this way is illustrated by the assessment of one of the children in our study. Following Robin's permanent exclusion from school for aggressive behaviour towards his teachers the local authority had to decide whether or not to initiate formal assessment procedures under the 1981 Act. While the education authority were considering their actions Robin, who was 15, was temporarily taken into the care of the local authority, pending a full court hearing. At a case conference called by the education authority, to which representatives of the social services department were invited, the discussion focused upon the type of provision that would be appropriate. His teachers made it clear that they would not accept him back into school. However, the educational psychologist was unwilling to recommend a special school placement. He argued that there was evidence that Robin had a very high academic ability and, this being the case, the curriculum of most special schools would be inappropriate for Robin's academic needs. On the other hand, he acknowledged that if an alternative mainstream placement was to be successfully negotiated then obtaining a care order was essential. Without this it was unlikely that any mainstream head teacher could be persuaded to accept Robin once they became aware of his difficult home circumstances.

Robin's social worker was concerned about Robin's home situation and identified the importance of removing him from this 'disturbed' environment as his main priority. Yet he had doubts about the ability of his department to act effectively in this case because 'our evidence might not stand up in a court'. He tried, therefore, to persuade the education authority that Robin's needs would best be served by a placement in a residential special school made under a Statement of special educational needs.

It is this Department's belief that in order to meet Robin's educational and behavioural needs he is in need of an *educational placement* which will provide the opportunity for Robin to meet his academic potential together with a stable, disciplined home environment where clear control and structure is provided.

The psychologist accepted that Robin's home environment was detrimental to his well being but believed that a special school placement would only add to his adjustment difficulties in the longer term. Moreover, he argued that if a care order were to be made by the court in respect of Robin then social services would have the main responsibility for him and would therefore have 'ownership of the problem', including the financial implications. In these circumstances the educational psychologist refused to initiate the Statementing procedures as an *alternative to care*.

Until you get the care order Education has no brief. That's all we can say until you [social services] have made the final decision.

From the perspective of Robin's social workers this suggestion merely delayed the inevitability of the decisions that would have to be taken, but it was also a source of frustration because in the absence of a care order their hands were tied. Without the care order they recognised that they would have to 'work very closely with education' to have any chance of securing their own objectives.

At the outset of discussions between social workers and education professionals the concern of the former was not merely that of protecting what they saw as the interests of the child but also that of finding ways to 'free up' the decision-making power of their own department. The attempt to obtain a care order was made with three considerations in mind.

1. A belief that Robin was trapped within a 'family pathology' that was inducing his own 'pathological behaviour'.
2. The ineffectiveness of interventions by the social services department with the family because Robin's parents (and Robin himself) did not share the social workers' perceptions of Robin's needs.
3. The difficulty they were experiencing in their negotiations with other agencies given the lack of any real authority to legitimise their involvement (as would have been provided if Robin was in care or if the social work intervention had been directed towards supporting Robin in his family).

In the absence of a care order the options for intervention available to social services were limited. However, this made conflict with the education authority more, rather than less, pronounced. The education authority was seen by the social services department as having the authority to act (under the Statementing procedures) and having access to resources that could be made available to meet Robin's needs. To secure these resources for Robin, his social workers believed it to be necessary to negotiate a definition of Robin's special educational needs in terms of his social and emotional interests. With this in mind they obtained a report on Robin from a psychologist employed by their department. This report identified Robin as suffering from an emotional and psychiatric disturbance requiring specialist treatment. If the LEA accepted this 'diagnosis' Robin's social workers believed there would be little chance of finding a mainstream school willing to accept him, leaving residential school as the only option available to the LEA.

Not surprisingly, the suggestion that Robin's behaviour was the product of a psychiatric disorder was vehemently contested by the educational psychologist. The latter argued that this diagnosis was incorrect and that Robin's behaviour was no more than a severe conduct order, albeit the product of a 'pathological family background'. Once removed from this environment, he argued, Robin's behaviour would improve and his educational needs would be manageable within a mainstream school.

Although at one level the issue here is about resources, it is clearly also about the authority of professional judgements. Thus, the educational psychologist was adamant that when assessed by social services Robin would have been

seen by unqualified psychologists who might have a degree in psychology but [who] don't have any professional training.

The educational psychologist's claim to greater professional authority was subsequently used by him to legitimise his power to dismiss the judgement of his colleagues in the social services department and to override their recommendations:

Well, they can assess him but it doesn't mean we have to act upon it. I have the advantage that I write the Statement.

As the LEA's representative in its negotiations with social services, the educational psychologist was unwilling to commit the LEA resources to the very different priorities of the social services department, but the effect of doing so in this case would also have been to undermine the authority of his professional role in the 1981 Act assessment procedures.

The negotiations between psychologist and social workers focused on two questions: first, that of which agency had the principal responsibility for Robin and therefore in what terms his needs were to be defined and prioritised; second, how, and by whom, resources could be released to meet the needs that had been identified in answer to the first question.

When, some months later, a care order was finally obtained by the social services department the relationship between professionals from the different agencies working with Robin became less fraught. In part, this reflected a recognition by these agencies of the ways in which the conflict between them had contributed to their mutual ineffectiveness. However, it also reflected a new understanding of Robin's needs based upon a clearer demarcation of responsibilities. The fact that the social services department was now able to employ its own resources to match and support those it was still seeking from the education authority facilitated a mutual recognition on the part of the two departments that their previous inability to resolve their disagreements had arisen, in part at least, from the inequality of their respective negotiating positions. Now, according to Robin's social worker, it was possible

to define roles so that everything is being considered and not duplicated.

Conclusions

In this chapter we have argued that there is little evidence of multidisciplinary collaboration in the assessment of children with special educational needs. This is despite the emphasis the 1981 Education Act places on identifying the needs of the whole child. Research evidence reviewed in this chapter suggests that, in practice, multidisciplinary cooperation tends to be restricted to the completion of bureaucratic procedures rather than any genuine attempt at what Goacher *et al.* (1988) referred to as 'collective multiprofessional assessment'. Professionals belonging to each of the disciplines involved in assessments under the 1981 Act, for the most part, perceive the multidisciplinary component of the assessment in these terms. This may be seen as reflecting the clear demarcation of roles and responsibilities that informs the participation of different professionals in these procedures. We have argued that exceptions to this occur where this demarcation of professional roles and responsibilities is unclear. In these cases the significance of the multidisciplinary component of an assessment will be enhanced. However, the focus for negotiations taking place about a child's needs are likely to centre upon the ownership of clients and the ownership and control of resources rather than simply upon the needs of the child as such.

The breakdown of the multidisciplinary model for assessing children's special educational needs arises because the model – at least in the form advocated by the Warnock Report and implemented in the 1981 Education Act – fails to recognise and understand properly the relationship between assessment and decision-making. It is naively assumed in the 1981 Act that the function of assessment is to identify, in some independent and objective sense, the needs of the whole child and that this assessment process will be carried out by professionals who have no interest in the outcome other than that of providing an objective assessment.

Decision-making about how the needs that have been identified should be met, if at all, is seen as a separate, administrative process. However, as we have argued, professional judgements do not simply arise out of clinical assessments. Clinical criteria are difficult, probably impossible, to define. Indeed, the philosophy of the 1981 Act, with its emphasis upon the interactive nature of needs, is at odds with any attempt to apply prescriptive criteria in each and every case. In these circumstances, the social character of the assessment can be seen. It is a process in which decisions are negotiated between professionals, as well as between professionals and their 'clients', in pursuit of a range of professional, political and pragmatic objectives (among which can be included a humanitarian concern that the best possible outcome should be reached for the child). The primary role of multidisciplinary assessment, whatever the ideals of its advocates, is to provide an arena for these negotiations.

CHAPTER 10

Conclusions

Introduction

Rutter *et al.* (1970) saw 'maladjustment' as an administrative concept, useful principally for arranging admissions to special schools. The term has never been used in any widely recognised classification system in child psychiatry. The 1981 Act abolished the categories of handicap recognised under the 1944 Education Act, but the introduction and widespread use of the expression EBD showed the difficulty in abandoning categories. Special schools and units continued to specialise in the education of children with difficult behaviour. Teachers in mainstream schools continued to find them disturbing. Developing a verbal shorthand to describe common understanding – or at least to describe what the people concerned assume to be common understanding – is part of all social experience. Jargon is merely one form of verbal shorthand, occurring when a professional group uses it in a way that excludes other groups from the discourse.

Nevertheless, both professionals and the public need a way of talking about specialist resources, whether services such as physio- or speech-therapy, or schools specialising in the education of particular groups of children. EBD is as much an administrative construct as maladjustment, and has no more clinical or descriptive validity. Yet if it falls out of favour, the one thing of which we can be certain is that, like maladjustment, it will rapidly be replaced by something equally problematic.

EBD then, is essentially a form of verbal shorthand, referring to children with widely different needs whose common characteristic is their disturbing behaviour, used to facilitate inter- and intraprofessional discussion and administrative decision-making. Like any other such term it has social origins, and its assessment is a social process. As our research shows, this involves a wide range of people with different and often conflicting hopes, fears and expectations.

In this final chapter we shall consider whether it is realistic to aim at consistency in policy and practice. We shall ask whether independence and fairness is in fact possible, and shall suggest that many of the anomalies we have identified arise from the extended definition of special educational needs originating in the Warnock Report. Finally, we shall argue that good practice in special educational provision, as in every aspect of education, has an ideological and philosophical basis, and that if we are serious about developing assessment processes which are helpful to children, parents *and* teachers, we shall have to base them on a shared and negotiated understanding of good practice.

Is consistency in policy and practice possible?

The partnership envisaged in the 1944 Act between schools, LEAs and government was overturned by the reforms of the 1980s and early 1990s. Power moved dramatically towards the centre and, in a superficial sense, to school governors. LEAs were increasingly emasculated, and the National Curriculum imposed a straitjacket on curriculum content. Nevertheless, LEAs retained responsibility for some provision, and even if they are eventually phased out, as envisaged in the 1993 Act, some alternative structure will be needed to administer this.

From the perspective of teachers, the reforms of the 1980s and early 1990s took place in a cold economic climate. Resources appeared to be either static or declining. Even though government figures purported to show an increase in overall expenditure on education, the reality for class teachers was all too often one of rapid curricular reform with insufficient time or resources to sustain it, combined with increased expectations from parents and governors. The increase in referrals of children with EBD for formal assessment under the 1981 Act almost certainly reflects the pressures which teachers feel themselves to be under rather than any absolute increase in problem behaviour. Yet it is in provision for children with SEN that demand for additional resources has most obviously outstripped supply. In such circumstances conflict is inevitable. Only at the most superficial level is this conflict between parents and professionals. Rather, it is between different professional groups, each of which quite legitimately has its own priorities and agenda. Head teachers are necessarily concerned about the stability of the school and its reputation in the local community. Class teachers are necessarily concerned about the progress of the majority of children in their class. Both head and class teachers are likely to have a genuine concern for the welfare and educational progress of the child with EBD, but this concern *must* be tempered by wider considerations. LEA officers have different priorities, namely finding an equitable way of allocating finite resources between a seemingly infinite number of demands. Parents, inevitably and rightly, have a much clearer priority, namely their child's welfare. In principle, this is also the first concern of educational psychologists, but the ambiguity of their role as LEA employees providing a service to schools creates conflicting pressures.

Conflict is inevitable in any situation in which demand for

resources exceeds supply. It is also inevitable when individuals approach assessment of a child's needs from different perspectives and with different priorities. Conflict can be resolved in ways that prove satisfactory to no participants, to some or to all. 'Good' conflict resolution is not impossible in a climate which recognises and respects the conflicting perspectives of the various parties. Two obvious questions arise. The first is whether legislation in Britain aggravates or reduces problems in finding solutions acceptable to class teachers, head teachers, parents and children. The second, and more complex, question is whether current legislation is being implemented in a political and educational climate which aggravates or reduces these problems.

Like the Warnock Report, the 1981 Act was based on the principle of professional consensus. It enabled parents to be involved in most stages of their children's assessment and gave them the right of appeal against professional decisions. A close look at the wording of the Act suggests that these rights of appeal may carry little weight in practice. For example, Galloway and Goodwin (1987) argued that the conditions for attendance at a mainstream school were so stringent that no child was ever placed at any special school under the 1944 Act who would not have been caught by at least one of them. Yet the Act both reflected and contributed to a new climate. Whereas the 1944 Act required children with a recognised category of handicap to be placed in a special school unless the circumstances were exceptional, the 1981 Act required them to be taught in the mainstream unless the circumstances were exceptional. For children with sensory and/or physical disabilities this resulted in greater integration, largely though by no means entirely at parents' request. For children with EBD it did not.

There is no evidence that the increase in specialist provision for children and young people with behavioural problems resulted from parents putting pressure on professionals to have them removed from the mainstream. Our own research suggests the reverse. Pressure for their removal did exist, but came principally from teachers who were struggling to cope with rapid curriculum changes. Hence, 12 of the 29 children whose assessment we followed were excluded indefinitely either before their assessment started or while it was in progress.

This raised an interesting question about the effect of LEA policy in allocating resources. In the LEA attended by seven of the excluded children, recommendations by educational psychologists for residential special school placement were routinely accepted. As they made clear in interviews with us, psychologists recognised that they had little option but to recommend residential school once a child had been excluded; schools were not enthusiastic about accepting each other's problems. Residential schooling cost this LEA around £20,000 annually for each pupil. Yet the LEA's 'generosity' in allocating such massive resources to EBD resulted in many parents feeling that they were being coerced into accepting something they did not want. For the price of placing a child in a residential school the LEA could have offered the child's school an additional teacher working almost full time to help support him or her in the mainstream. Such an offer, however, was considered out of the question. Galloway (1990c) has described a similar situation in a London Borough which was placing large numbers of children in out-of-city schools. Towards the end of our research, the LEA with the highest number of exclusions found itself in financial problems. As a result, the chief education officer was instructed by his council to scrutinise personally each recommendation in order to cut down the costs. Suddenly, mainstream provision became available for a young person who had previously been considered totally unplaceable.

In spite of their unhappiness about the outcome of their children's assessments it was striking that no parents in the study exercised their rights of appeal against professional decisions. Nor did any of them contemplate litigation. The 1981 Act never led to the flood of court cases that followed the equivalent legislation in the United States, Public Law 94/142. The reasons lie partly in differences between the two legal systems, partly in the fact that few parents in our study could have contemplated legislation without legal aid, which would almost certainly not have been available, and partly in the wording of the Act itself which severely restricts the grounds for litigation.

Legal challenges, then, are unlikely to be helpful in revealing anomalies in legislation for special educational provision. To understand why the experience of assessment is often stressful for all involved – teachers, other professionals, parents and children – we have to look at the wider picture. Returning to our argument in Chapter 1, legislation for SEN is based on the 'special needs pupil' discourse at a time when initially all other educational legislation is prompted by the 'school failure' discourse. This creates two peculiarly intransigent difficulties.

1. Assessment all too easily becomes divorced from wider considerations of school and teacher effectiveness, concentrating on what is wrong with children or their families rather than on ways in which they could be taught effectively within the ordinary classroom. There is an interesting parallel here with US Public Law 94/162. Owing to the litigious climate in the United States, there has been a tendency for professionals to take the 'safe' option of recommending a programme specially designed for the individual child, rather than the more 'risky' option of a programme based on the teacher's regular work with the class. Thus, a time of unparalleled demand for children with learning difficulties to be brought into the mainstream witnessed an unparalleled increase in the number of children being withdrawn from mainstream classes for special help. The reason could hardly

have been educational, since the long-term limitations of specialist 'remedial' help were well known. It is, however, much more difficult to prove negligence if special help has been provided on an individual or small group basis than if no such help has been offered.

2.   Assessment can be seen as a way of reducing pressures on teachers who are concerned about their school's public image. At a time of sustained criticism from Tory politicians that schools do too little to maintain high standards of behaviour, and fail to meet the educational needs of many of their pupils, it is scarcely surprising that teachers should see assessment as a way of 'proving' that a child has SEN which cannot reasonably be met in the mainstream without special help.

This occurs, however, largely because of the extended concept of SEN proposed in the Warnock Report and accepted in the subsequent legislation. By extending the concept to include 20 per cent of pupils, or 50 per cent if we accept the view of HMI in Scotland (SED, 1978), Warnock and the 1981 Act brought SEN into the political arena of school and teacher effectiveness. Unfortunately, they did so without acknowledging that the ideology behind their proposals was based on the 'special needs pupil' discourse. At any other time, this might not have mattered. Coming, as it did, at a time of sustained political attacks on the education system, and in particular on the quality of schools' work with below-average pupils, together with other additional demands on resources, it was a recipe for frustration, bitterness and confrontation. LEAs found themselves responsible for meeting intensified needs without the powers to do so in an effective way. The government had the power to increase resources for SEN, but washed its hands of responsibility for a situation of its own making, preferring to lay the blame for any problems on the LEAs whose powers it had removed. Parents and children were the jam in an unpalatable sandwich.

Can assessment be 'independent' and 'fair'?

We have already argued that educational psychologists cannot be expected to assess children's needs without reference to the resources available for meeting them. Legislation for SEN provision is nevertheless based on the principle that assessment should not only be independent but also fair. This leaves two questions: independent from what?, and fair to whom? In their interviews with us, head teachers and class teachers expressed with considerable integrity the dilemma they faced. There were considerations which extended beyond the children who were being assessed, and these considerations were relevant both to the children's problems and to the support the school felt able to give them. Yet reports focused largely on the child's difficulties, with little reference to the other matters that emerged in discussion with the research team. This was perhaps inevitable. Ideas expressed in a one-to-one interview can be difficult to commit to paper; moreover, the relationships between a child's emotional and behavioural difficulties and a teacher's classroom effectiveness is invariably both complex and speculative: it is better to confine the issue to a description of the child's behaviour and progress.

For educational psychologists the problem was similar. They could only carry out a 'fair' assessment if they knew the strengths and weaknesses of the school and the child's class. This required that they should have worked closely with teachers in the school, but there was a sense in which that in itself could weaken their independence in carrying out an assessment of the child. The more closely they had worked with teachers, the more likely they might be to see the problem from the teacher's perspective and the less likely, perhaps, to see it from that of the child or parent.

LEA officers had to act on the advice received in allocating resources. This gave them an obvious independence that the professionals who were more directly involved often lacked. It was striking, though, that both the amount and the quality of advice varied from child to child. So did the power and influence of the advisers. One case was rapidly resolved when an MP took an interest. With the best will in the world, fairness could be little more than an aspiration.

Is there a way through this tangle? We believe that there is, but only if the government is prepared to acknowledge that Warnock's notion of 20 per cent of children having SEN at some time in their school career has outlived its usefulness. The crucial question concerns the proportion of children whom schools should be able to teach effectively without additional resources. This is essentially a political question. The reason is simply that the allocation of national resources to education must be a political responsibility.

Has Warnock's 20 per cent served its purpose?

The principle behind funding for SEN seems to us eminently defensible, namely that the school's annual budget under the LMS formula contains an element for provision for the majority of children with special needs, while the minority whose needs cannot be met from the school's own resources are catered for by means of provision specified in a Statement. The problem lies in the open-ended and non-specific criteria for issuing Statements. By failing to differentiate in any clear or coherent way between the minority of Warnock's 20 per cent who require a Statement and the majority who do not, legislation has created unresolvable tensions. In particular, it has enabled head teachers and governors to 'lose' the SEN element in the school's overall budget and to act as though special provision could only be provided through a Statement. Some LEA policies have compounded this problem by delegating relatively small proportions of the overall budget for SEN provision to schools, retaining expensive central support services which are not always responsive to the day-to-day problems which arise in schools.

If it were to be asserted categorically that schools should be expected to cater for a reasonably well-defined proportion of children without additional resources beyond those in their annual budget or available from LEA support services, discussion might more readily focus on the most effective ways of using these resources. Two questions arise: first, how should resources for children without statements be allocated to schools? and, second, for what proportion of children should LEAs be expected to issue Statements? We deal with these separately.

1. The DFE could give LEAs guidance on the proportion of the overall resources delegated to schools which are intended for SEN provision. If it were to be assumed that 20 per cent of pupils throughout the LEA might require some additional support, it would not be unreasonable to allocate 35 per cent of the overall budget to the education of these pupils, thus leaving 65 per cent for the remaining 80 per cent of pupils with no special needs or difficulties. The precise amount allocated to each school should, however, be weighted according to a formula agreed locally to take account of difference between schools in children's socio-economic background. Schools serving disadvantaged areas would receive more. LEAs should also receive guidance on the resources they should retain centrally for services to assist schools in developing their own policies and priorities with respect to SEN. Just as it is unrealistic to require head teachers to cater for pupils with learning or behavioural problems when they do not control the resources intended for these pupils, so it is equally unrealistic to expect them to respond effectively to special needs without access to specialist guidance and advice. Centrally funded services, however, would not be responsible for individual children; instead their function would be to help the school in developing its own responses to these children.

2. The DFE should advise LEAs that no more than 2 per cent of all children should receive Statements, and that no more than 1 per cent should receive Statements on account of EBD or moderate learning difficulties. This, of course, is roughly the proportion of children taught in special schools in classes prior to the 1981 Act. Nevertheless, our proposal that only 2 per cent of children should receive Statements is logically independent of the mainstream/special school debate. Indeed, we acknowledge that although the research has major limitations (Hornby, 1991), there appears to be

no evidence that the educational progress of children with learning difficulties is harmed by mainstream placement (Galloway and Goodwin, 1987). Thus, it would be as logical for children with Statements to be taught in a mainstream school as in a special school.

Whether it is morally acceptable to reduce the limited 'protection' offered by a Statement to a mere 2 per cent of children depends entirely on the quality of education available to the remaining 98 per cent, and the quality of information available to their parents. Any additional information about SEN, or additional provision based on this, cannot realistically be expected to be qualitatively different from what is provided for all children, but should rather be seen as a logical extension to it. In particular, it seems necessary that there should be a clear policy on:

(a) the progress reports that should be available for all children, and the relationships between them and National Curriculum testing programmes;
(b) the nature of assessment that should be carried out when teachers *or* parents suspect that a child may be having learning difficulties;
(c) the right of parents to participate in the assessment;
(d) the information to be made available to them;
(e) teachers' and governors' accountability to parents and to independent inspection teams for the use of funds intended for SEN provision;
(f) schools being required to delegate resources to LEAs in respect of pupils they are unable to teach themselves; but who do not qualify for a Statement.

Overview

This book has addressed the question of the assessment process for one particular kind of designated 'special need'. Yet we pointed out in chapter 1 that SEN is a deeply ambiguous and confused concept. How do we know when a 'special' need is a normal response to abnormal circumstances? How do we disentangle the educational and social needs of children from the needs of parents, teachers, schools and the wider society? We have shown that the question of whose special needs are really being served by the concept and by the assessment process still remains problematic.

It is perhaps too easy to criticise the policies that have contributed to many of the tensions in the assessment of SEN identified in our research – for example, the crude league tables of school performance, the politicisation of the curriculum, the emasculation of LEAs and the seemingly interminable attacks on teachers and other educationalists.

The fact nevertheless remains that no government can legislate for good practice nor for goodwill. The debate on what politicians and parents should expect of schools in relation to SEN provision is logically independent of any policy on Statementing, but it is integrally linked to notions of good practice.

What is regarded as good practice varies across cultures and across time. The principle of curriculum entitlement for *all* pupils, backed by information from regular assessments of their progress, indicates one approach to good practice. Similarly, publicly available information on school performance indicators, including details of pupils' performance in national testing programmes, reflect 'official' views of good practice. These, however, are based on notional evidence of good practice, and not on the process which illustrates it. This is even more contentious, since it is linked not just to measurable outcomes such as educational progress but to less tangible outcomes such as the school's influence on the child's social adjustment, personality and behaviour – in short, the sort of person he or she becomes.

Good practice is a notoriously slippery concept. Some politicians seem to regard it in infant schools as phonic drill, insistence on children speaking standard English and an introduction to grammar. Yet the same politicians who deride the so-called 'Real Books' approach to reading in favour of phonics, applaud Marie Clay's (1985) Reading Recovery scheme which is based on children learning to read 'real books'. Similarly, the DES has advocated extending the concept of partnership to children and young people in the assessment of SEN, while the 1986 Education Act proscribed school governors extending the concept of partnership to older students by co-opting them on to the Governing Body.

What emerges from our research is that agreement on good practice in provision for SEN can only be based on a dialogue between all who are involved in children's education: teachers, other professionals, parents and the students themselves. That, however, is a value judgement which would be indignantly refuted in many quarters. Indeed, Mary Warnock (1985) cautioned against her own Committee's earlier commitment to the principle of partnership with parents, arguing that in some matters parents could never be the equal of teachers. Had she been prepared to acknowledge that the reverse was also true – namely, that parents' knowledge of their own child is in some respects greater than that of teachers and that parents often have knowledge of matters which may exert a profound influence on a child's progress and adjustment at school – her highly publicised Dimbleby Lecture might have been more illuminating.

At present, assessment is too often a harrowing experience for everyone concerned: for teachers who feel under stress at a time of increasing demands, for LEA officers at a time of diminishing powers, for educational psychologists who find themselves serving people with incompatible interests, for parents and children who feel caught in a web that they cannot fully understand, let alone break through. The tensions inherent in assessment of SEN under current legislation reflect wider tensions in an education system that is being subjected to radical change. In acknowledging these tensions, however, we should never lose sight of the clear evidence from research on school and teacher effectiveness as well as from HMI reports that individual schools are consistently providing high-quality education for their most vulnerable and disturbing pupils. Moreover, within most schools there are teachers who achieve similarly high standards. The fact that so many teachers and other professionals are able to work successfully with a system so beset by internal anomalies and contradictions does not reduce the need for reform of that system; but it does provide grounds for optimism.

BIBLIOGRAPHY

Alexander, R., Rose, J. and Woodhead, C. (1992) *Curriculum Organisation and Classroom Practice in Primary Schools: A Discussion Paper*. London, Department of Education and Science.

Allen, C.V. (1980) *Daddy's Girl: A Very Personal Memoir*. Toronto, McClelland and Stewart-Bantam.

Apple, M. (1982) *Cultural and Economic Reproduction in Education: Essays on Class, Ideology and the State*. London, Routledge and Kegan Paul.

Armstrong, D. and Galloway, D. (1992a) Who is the child psychologists' client? Responsibilities and options for psychologists in Educational Settings. *Association for Child Psychology and Psychiatry Newsletter*, **14** (2) 62–6.

Armstrong, D. and Galloway, D. (1992b) On being a client: conflicting perspectives for assessment. In T. Booth, W. Swann, M. Masterton, and P. Potts. *Learning for All. 2: Policies for Diversity in Education*. London, Routledge and Kegan Paul.

Armstrong, D., Galloway, D. and Tomlinson, S. (1991) Decision-making in psychologists' professional interviews. *Educational Psychology in Practice*, **7** (2), 82–7.

Armstrong, D., Galloway, D and Tomlinson, S. (1993) Assessing special educational needs: the child's cost: *British Educational Research Journal*, **19**, 121–131.

Armstrong, L. (1978) *Kiss Daddy Goodnight: A Speak-Out on Incest*. New York, Pocket Books.

Association of Educational Psychologists (1984) *Members Handbook*. London, AEP.

Audit Commission and Her Majesty's Inspectorate (AC–HMI) (1992) *Getting in on the Act. Provision for Pupils with Special Educational Needs: The National Picture*. London, HMSO.

Bagley, C. (1982) Achievement, behaviour disorder and social circumstances in West Indian children and other ethnic groups. In G.K. Verma, and C. Bagley. *Self-Concept and Multicultural Education*. London, Macmillan.

Ball, S.J. (1981) *Beachside Comprehensive*. Cambridge, Cambridge University Press.

Barrett, M. (1986) *From Education to Segregation – An Inquiry into the Changing Character of Special Provision for the Retarded in England 1846–1918. Unpublished PhD Dissertation. Lancaster, University of Lancaster.*

Barton, L. and Meighan R. (1979) *Schools, Pupils and Deviance*. Driffield, Nafferton Books.

Barton, L. and Tomlinson S. (eds) (1984) *Special Education and Social Interests*. London, Croom Helm.

Bennett, T.N., Desforges, C., Cockburn, A. and Wilkinson B. (1984) *The Quality of Pupil Learning Experiences*. London, Lawrence Earlbaum.

Blishen, E. (1955) *Roaring Boys*. London, Thames and Hudson.

Boardieu, P. (1977) Cultural Reproduction and Social Reproduction. In J. Karabel and A.H. Halsey (eds) *Power and Ideology in Education*, New York, Oxford University Press.

Board of Education and Board of Control (BoE/BoC) (1929) *Report of the Joint Departmental Committee on Mental Deficiency* (The Wood Committee). London, HMSO.

Bogdan, B. and Kugelmass, J. (1984) Case studies of mainstreaming: a symbolic-interactionist approach. In L. Barton and S. Tomlinson *Special Education and Social Interests*. London, Croom Helm.

Bond, L. and Compas, B. (eds) (1989) *Primary Prevention and Promotion in the Schools*. Newbury Park, California, Sage.

Booth, T. and Statham, J. (eds) (1982) *The Nature of Special Education*. Milton Keynes, Open University Press.

Bowles, S. and Gintis, H. (1976) *Schooling in Capitalist America*. London, Routledge and Kegan Paul.

Boyson, R. (1988) Follow the Lewes Priory Four. *Times Educational Supplement*, 18 March, p. 4.

Brady, K. (1979) *Father's Days: A True Story of Incest*. New York, Dell.

Broadfoot, P. (ed.) (1986) *Profiles and Records of Achievement: A Review of Issues and Practices*. London, Holt, Rinehart and Winston.

Burgess, R.G. (1983) *Experiencing Comprehensive Education*. London, Methuen.

Butler-Sloss, E. (1988) *Report of the Inquiry into Child Abuse in Cleveland in 1987*. London, HMSO.

Callaghan, J. (1976) *Speech by the Prime Minister*, the Rt Hon. James Callaghan MP, at a foundation stone laying ceremony at Ruskin College, Oxford, on Monday, 18 October (press release).

Cameron, A.C. (1931) *Education and the Retarded Child*. Paper to members and officers of LEA's. Great Yarmouth. 7 April 1931.

Central Advisory Council for Education (CACE) (1967) *Children and their Primary Schools* (The Plowden Report). London, HMSO.

Chaudhury, A. (1986) *Annual Report of Advisory Centre for Education*. London, ACE.

Childright (1991) Centre calls for Act with more right. *Childright*, **82**, 7.

Clay, M. (1985) *The Early Detection of Reading Difficulties* (3rd edn) Auckland, New Zealand, Heinemann.

Coleman, J.S. *et al.* (1966) *Equality of Educational Opportunity*. Washington, US Government Printing Office.

Commission for Racial Equality (CRE) (1985) *Birmingham Local Education Authority and Schools: Referral and Suspension of Pupils*. London, CRE.

Cooper, P., Upton, G., and Smith, C. (1991) Ethnic minority and gender distribution among staff and pupils in facilities for pupils with emotional and behavioural disorders in England and Wales. *British Journal of Sociology of Education*, **12**, 77–94.

Corrigan, P. (1979) *Schooling the Smash Street Kids*. London, Macmillan.

Cox, B. (1991) *Cox on Cox: An English Curriculum for the 1990s*. London, Hodder and Stoughton.

Cox, C.B. and Boyson, R. (1977) *Black Paper, 1977*. London, Morris Temple Smith.

Cross, C. and Gallagher, C. (eds) (1990) Special issue on the new Children Act. *Maladjustment and Therapeutic Education*, **8** (iii) 121–178.

Davies, D. (1991) *The Effect of Certain Sections of the Children Act 1989 on Residential Schools for Emotionally and Behaviourally Disturbed Children*. Unpublished MA Dissertation, Lancaster University.

Dean, C. (1992) Troublesome pupils cannot be sifted out. *Times Educational Supplement*, 3rd July, 1992.

Department of Education and Science (DES) (1975) *The Discovery of Children Requiring Special Education and the Assessment of their Needs* (Circular 2/75). London, DES.

Department of Education and Science (DES) (1978) *Special Educational Needs* (The Warnock Report). London, HMSO.

Department of Education and Science (DES) (1983) *Assessments and Statements of Special Educational Needs* (Circular 1/83), London, DES.

Department of Education and Science (DES) (1989a) *Assessments and Statements of Special Educational Needs: Procedures within the Education, Health and Social Services* (Circular 22/89). London, DES.

Department of Education and Science (DES) (1989b) *Discipline in Schools* (The Elton Report). London, HMSO.

Department of Education and Science (DES) (1989c) *Education Reform Act 1988: Temporary Exceptions from the National Curriculum* (Circular 15/89). London: DES

Department of Education and Science and Her Majesty's Inspector of Schools (DES, HMI) (1990) *Educational Psychology Services in England 1988–1989*. London, HMSO.

Department of Further Education (DFE) Exclusions: a Discussion Paper. London, HMSO.

Department of Health and Social Security (DHSS) (1976) *Fit for the Future* (The Court Report). London, HMSO.

Douglas, J.W.B. (1964) *The Home and the School*. London, MacGibbon and Kee.

Dupont, S. and Dowdney, L. (1990a) Dilemmas in working with schools. *Association for Child Psychology and Psychiatry Newsletter*, **12** (i), 13–16.

Dupont, S. and Dowdney, L. (1990b) Letters to the Editors. *Association for Child Psychology and Psychiatry Newsletter*, **12** (iii), 41–2.

Dyson, S. (1986) Professionals, mentally handicapped children and confidential files. *Disability, Handicap and Society*, **1**, 73–87.

Education (1978) Warnock reactions. *Education*, 2 June, p. 490.

Etzioni, A. (ed.) (1969) *The Semi-Professions and their Organisation*. New York, Free Press.

Faunce, W. and Clellan, D.A. (1967) Professionalization and stratification patterns in an industrial community. *American Journal of Sociology*, **72**, 341–52.

Fontana, D. (1984) Failures of academic achievement. In A. Gale and A.J. Chapman (eds) *Psychology and Social Problems*. London, Macmillan/BPS.

Ford, J., Mongon, D. and Whelan, M. (1982) *Special Education and Social Control*. London, Routledge.

Freeman, M.D.A. (1987) Taking children's rights seriously. *Children and Society*, **1**, 299–319.

Fulcher, G. (1989) *Disabling Policies – a comparative approach to educational policy and disability*. Lewes, Falmer Press.

Galloway, D. (1985) *Schools, Pupils and Special Educational Needs*. London, Croom Helm.

Galloway, D. (1990a) Was the GERBIL a Marxist mole? In P. Evans and V. Varma (eds) *Special Education: Past, Present and Future*. Lewes, Falmer Press.

Galloway, D. (1990b) Who is the Client? *Letters to the Editors, Association for Child Psychology and Psychiatry Newsletter*, **12** (iii), 40–1.

Galloway, D. (1990c) *Ealing's Opportunity*? Report of the Consultant on Special Educational Needs. London, Ealing Education Department.

Galloway, D. and Goodwin, C. (1979) *Educating Slow Learning and Maladjusted Children: Integration or Segregation*? London, Longman.

Galloway, D. and Goodwin, C. (1987) *The Education of Disturbing Children: Pupils with Learning and Adjustment Difficulties*. London, Longman.

Galloway, D., Tomlinson, S. and Armstrong, D. (1991) *The Identification of Emotional and Behavioural Difficulties: Participant Perspectives*. (Final Report to the Economic ans Social Research Council, grant No. R000 231393.) Swindon, ESRC.

Galloway, D., Ball, T., Blomfield, D. and Seyd, R. (1982) *Schools and Disruptive Pupils*. London, Longman.

Galloway, D., Wilcox, B. and Martin, R. (1985) Persistent absence from school and exclusion from school: the predictive power of school and community variables. *British Educational Research Journal*, **11**, 51–61.

Gardner, R. (1985) Client participation in decision-making in child care: a review of research. *Highlight*, **71**, National Children's Bureau.

Gardner, R. (1987) *Who Says? Choice and Control in Care*. London, National Children's Bureau.

Garforth, D. (1986) Instituting records of achievement at county level: the Dorset/Southern Regional Examinations Board Assessment and Profiling Project. In P. Broadfoot (ed) *Profiles and Records of Achievement: A Review of Issues and Practices*. London, Holt, Rinehart and Winston.

Gath, D., Cooper, B., Gattoni, F. and Rockett, D. (1977) *Child Guidance and Delinquency in a London Borough*. Oxford, Oxford University Press.

Gersch, I.S. (1987) Involving pupils in their own assessment. In T. Bowers (ed.) *Special Educational Needs and Human Resource Management*. London, Croom Helm.

Gersch, I.S. (1990) The pupil's view. In M. Scherer, I.S. Gersch, and L. Fry (eds) *Meeting Disruptive Behaviour, Assessment, Interaction and Partnerships*. London, Macmillan.

Gillham, B. (1978) *Reconstructing Educational Psychology*. London, Croom Helm.

Gillick vs West Norfolk and Wisbech Area Health Authority (1986), 1 FLR 224.

Giroux, H. (1983) *Theory and Resistance in Education: A Pedagogy for the Opposition*. New York, Heineman.

Goacher, B., Evans, Welton, J. and Wedell, K. (1988) *Policy and Provision for Special Educational Needs: Implementing the 1981 Education Act*. London, Cassell.

Graham, P. and Rutter, M. (1970) Selection of children with psychiatric disorder. In M. Rutter, J. Tizard and K. Whitmore (eds) *Education, Health and Behaviour*. London, Longman.

Grace, G. (1987) Teachers and the State in Britain: a changing relation. In M. Lawn and G. Grace (eds) *Teachers: the Culture and Politics of Work*. Lewes, Falmer Press.

Habermas, J. (1974) *Theory and Practice*. London, Heinemann.

Hannam, C. (1975) *Parents and Mentally Handicapped Children*. Harmondsworth, Penguin.

Haggerty, M.E. (1925) The incidence of undesirable behaviour in public-school children. *Journal of Educational Research*, **12**, 102–22.

Hargreaves, D.H. (1967) *Social Relationships in a Secondary School*. London, Routledge and Kegan Paul.

Hargreaves, D.H. (1982) *The Challenge of the Comprehensive School: Culture, Curriculum, Community*. London, Routledge and Kegan Paul.

Hargreaves, D.H., Hestor, S.K. and Mellow, F.J. (1975) *Deviance in Classrooms*. London, Routledge and Kegan Paul.

Haviland, D. (1988) *Take Care, Mr. Baker!* London, Fourth Estate.

Hearnshaw, L.S. (1979) *Cyril Burt: Psychologist*. London, Hodder and Stoughton.

House of Commons (HC) (1987) *Special Educational Needs: Implementation of the Education Act 1981*. Third Report from the House of Commons Education, Science and Arts Committee. (Appendix E to the DES Evidence.) London, HMSO.

Hurt, J.S. (1988) *Outside the Mainstream*. London, Routledge and Kega n Paul.

Inner London Education Authority (ILEA) (1976) *William Tyndale Junior and Infants Schools Public Inquiry: A Report to the Inner London Education Authority* (The Auld Report). London, ILEA.

Inner London Education Authority (ILEA) (1984) *Improving Secondary Schools* (The Hargreaves Report). London, ILEA.

Inner London Education Authority (ILEA) (1985) *Equal Opportunities for All?* (The Fish Report). London, ILEA.

Jenkins, R. 1991. *Changing approaches to Mental Handicap*. Occasional Paper No. 3, School of Social Studies. Swansea, Swansea University College.

Joseph, K. (1983) *Address to Council of Local Education Authorities*, 16 July. Unpublished.

King, M. (1981) Are children's rights relevant? *Association of Educational Psychologists' Journal*, **5** (VI), 2–7.

Kirp, D. (1983) Professionalisation as a policy choice: British Special Education in corporative perspectives. In J.G. Chambers and W.T. Hartman (eds) *Special Education Policies – their History, Implementation and Finance*. Philadelphia, Temple University Press.

Klein, R. (1992) Is this what your child sees? *The Independent*, 13/2/92.

Kugelmass, J.W. (1987) *Behaviour, Bias and Handicap*. Oxford, Transaction Books.

Lacey, C. (1970) *Hightown Grammar: The School as a Social System*. Manchester, Manchester University Press.

Larson, M.S. (1977) *The Rise of Professionalism – A Sociological Analysis*. Berkeley, University of California Press.

Lawn, M. and Ozga, J. (1988) The educational worker? A reassessment of teachers. In J. Ozga (ed.) *School Work: Approaches to the Labour Process of Teaching*. Milton Keynes, Open University Press.

Lazarson, M. (1983) The origins of special education. In J.G. Chambers and W.T. Hartman (eds) *Special Education Policies*. Philadelphia, Temple University Press.

Lee, T. (1990) *Carving Out the Cash for Schools: L.M.S. and the New ERA of Education*. Bath, Centre for Analysis of Social Policy, University of Bath.

Ling, R. and Davis, G. (1984) *A Survey of Off-site Units in England and Wales*. Birmingham, Polytechnic School of Education.

Little, A.W. (1985) A child's understanding of the causes of academic success and failure: a case study of British schoolchildren. *British Journal of Educational Psychology*, **55**, 11–12.

McFie, B.S. (1934) Behaviour and personality difficulties in school children. *British Journal of Educational Psychology*, **4**, 30–6.

Malek, M. (1989) *Making an Educational Statement? An Analysis of the Admission of Children with Emotional and Behavioural Difficulties to Residential Special Schools*. Bath, University of Bath/The Children's Society.

Ministry of Education (MoE) (1945) *Handicapped Pupils and School Health Service Regulations* (Statutory Rules and Orders, no. 1076). London, HMSO.

Ministry of Education (MoE) (1955) *Maladjusted Children* (The Underwood Report). London, Ministry of Education.

Ministry of Education (MoE) (1959) *The Handicapped Pupils and Special Schools Regulations* (Statutory Instruments, no. 365). London, HMSO.

Mortimore, P., Sammons, P., Stoll, L., Lewis, D. and Ecob, R. (1988) *School Matters: The Junior Years*. Wells, Open Books.

Nisbet, J. and Schucksmith, J. (1986) *Learning Strategies*. London, Routledge.

Nottingham County Council (NCC) (1990) *Pupil Exclusions from Nottingham Secondary Schools*. Nottingham County Council Education Department.

Norwich, B. (1990) *Reappraising Special Needs Education*. London, Cassell.

O'Keefe, D. (1987) Schools as self-seeking syndicates. *Economic Affairs*, April/May.

Ozga, J. and Lawn, M. (1981) *Teachers, Professionalism and Class: A Study of Organised Teachers*. Lewes, Falmer Press.

Parry-Jones (1991) But will they listen? *Childright*, **82**, 16–18.

Power, M.J., Benn, R.T. and Morris, J.M. (1972) Neighbourhood, school and juveniles before the courts. *British Journal of Criminology*, **12**, 111–32.

Prais, S.J. (1986) Educating for productivity: comparisons of Japanese and English schooling and vocational preparation. *Compare*, **16**, 121–47.

Prais, S.J. and Wagner, K. (1986) Schooling standards in England and Germany: some summary comparisons bearing on economic performance. *Compare*, **16**, 5–35.

Pritchard, D.E. (1963) *The Education of the Handicapped 1760–1960*. London, Routledge.

Pyke, N. (1990) Psychologist wins support for sacking. *Times Educational Supplement*, 20 July, p. 1.

Ravenette, A.T. (1977) Personal construct theory: an approach to the psychological investigation of children and young people. In D. Bannister (ed.) *New Perspectives in Personal Construct Theory*. London, Academic Press.

Rehal, A. (1989) Involving Asian parents in the statementing procedure – the way forward. *Educational Psychology in Practice*, **4**, 189–97.

Rosenbaum, M. and Newell, P. (1991) *Taking Children Seriously: A Proposal for a Children's Right's Commissioner*. London, Calouste Gulbenkian Foundation.

Reynolds, D. (1976) When pupils and teachers refuse a truce: the secondary school and the creation of delinquency. In G. Mungham and G. Pearson (eds) *Working Class Youth Culture*. London, Routledge and Kegan Paul.

Riddell, S., Dyer, S. and Thomson, G. (1990) Parents, professionals and social welfare models: the implementation of the Education (Scotland) Act 1981. *European Journal of Special Needs Education*, **5**, 96–110.

Rutter, M. and Graham, P. (1968) The reliability and validity of the psychiatric assessment of the child: I. Interview with the child. *British Journal of Psychiatry*, **114**, 563–79.

Rutter, M., B. Maughan, P. Mortimore and J. Ouston, (1979) *15,000 Hours: Secondary Schools and their Effects on Pupils*. London, Open Books.

Rutter, M., Tizard, J. and Whitmore, K. (1970) *Education, Health and Behaviour*. London, Longman.

Scottish Education Department (SED) (1978) *The Education of Pupils with Learning Difficulties in Primary and Secondary Schools: A Progress Report by Her Majesty's Inspectorate*. Edinburgh, HMSO.

Sharron, H. (1985) Needs must. *Times Educational Supplement*, 22 February.

Shaw, L. (1990) *Each Belongs: Integrated Education in Canada*. London, Centre for Studies on Integration in Education.

Sigmon, S. (1987) *Radical Analysis of Special Education*. Lewes, Falmer Press.

Simmons, K. (1986) Painful Extractions. *Times Educational Supplement*, 17 October.

Simon, B. (1989) *The Great Schooling Scandal*. London, Lawrence and Wishart.

Simon, B. (1992) *What Future for Education?* London, Lawrence and Wishart.

Skrtic, T.M. (1991) *Behind Special Education: A Critical Analysis of Professional Culture and School Organization*. Denver, Love Publishing Co.

Smith, D.J. and Tomlinson, S. (1989) *The School Effect: A Study of Multiracial Comprehensives*. London, Policy Studies Institute.

Soder, M. (1992) Disabilities as a social construct - the labelling approach re-visited. In T. Booth, V. Swan, M. Masterton, P. Potts (eds) *Policies for Diversity in Education*. London, Routledge.

Squibb, P. (1981) A theoretical structuralist approach to special education. In L. Barton and S. Tomlinson (eds) *Special Education Policy, Practices and Social Issues*. London, Croom Helm.

Swann, W. (1984) Conflict and control: some observations on parents and the integration of children with special educational needs. Paper presented at the *Annual Conference of the British Psychological Society, Education Section*, September.

Swann, W. (1985) Is the integration of children with special needs happening? An analysis of recent statistics of pupils in special schools. *Oxford Review of Education*, **11**, 3–18.

Swann, W. (1987) Statements of intent: an assessment of reality. In T. Booth and W. Swann (eds) *Including Children with Disabilities*. Milton Keynes, Open University Press.

Swann, W. (1989) *Segregation Statistics English LEAs 1988–91* London, Centre for Studies on Integration in Education.

Tammivaara, J. and Enright, D.S. (1986) On eliciting information with child informants. *Anthropology and Education Quarterly*, **17**, 218-38.

Tomlinson, S. (1981a) *Educational Subnormality: A Study in Decision-Making*. London, Routledge and Kegan Paul.

Tomlinson, S. (1981b) Professionals and ESN(M) education. In W. Swann (ed.) *The Practice of Special Education*. Oxford, Blackwell.

Tomlinson, S. (1982) *A Sociology of Special Education*. London, Routledge.

Trueba, H., Spindler, G. and Spindler, L. (eds) (1989) *What Do Anthropologists Have to Say About Dropouts? The First Centennial Conference on Children at Risk*. New York, Falmer Press.

Ward, E. (1984) *Father–Daughter Rape*. London, Women's Press.

Warnock, M. (1982) Introduction. In J. Welton, K. Wendell, and G. Vorhaus (eds) *Meeting Special Educational Needs: The 1981 Education Act and its Implications*. Bedford Way Papers 12. London, University of London Institute of Education.

Warnock, M. (1985) Teacher teach thyself (The 1985 Dimbleby Lecture). *The Listener*, 28 March, pp. 10–14.

White, P. (1988) The new right and parental choice. *Journal of Philosophy of Education*, **22**, 195–9.

White, R., Carr, P. and Lane, N. (1990) *A Guide to the Children Act 1989*. London, Butterworth.

Willis, P. (1977) *Learning to Labour: How Working Class Kids get Working Class Jobs*. Farnborough, Saxon House.

Wood, S. (1988) Parents: whose partners? In L. Bartol (ed.) *The Politics of Special Educational Needs*. London, Falmer Press.

Woods, P. (1979) *The Divided School*. London, Routledge and Kegan Paul.

Wright, C. (1986) School processes – an ethnographic study. In J.Eggleston, D. Dunn and M. Anjali (eds) *Education For Some*. Stoke-on-Trent, Trentham Books, pp. 127–77.

Wringe, C.A. (1973) Pupils' rights. *Journal of Philosophy of Education*, **7**, 103–15.

Ysseldyke, A. and Algozzine, R. (1982). *Critical Issues in Special and Remedial Education*. Boston, Houghton-Mifflin.

INDEX